TRUTH AND REALITY

TRUTH
AND REALITY

BY

OTTO RANK

---

*Authorized Translation from the German,
with a Preface and Introduction, by*

JESSIE TAFT

W·W·NORTON & COMPANY·INC·

NEW YORK

First published in the Norton Library 1978
by arrangement with Alfred A. Knopf, Inc.

W. W. Norton & Company, Inc. is also the publisher of the works of Erik H.
Erikson, Otto Fenichel, Karen Horney, Harry Stack Sullivan, and The Standard
Edition of the Complete Psychological Works of Sigmund Freud.

Truth and Reality. Translated by Jessie Taft. Published July 1936. Original title:
Wahrheit and Wirklichkeit, Entwurf Einer Philosophie des Seelischen.
Copyright 1929 by Franz Deuticke.

Library of Congress Cataloging in Publication Data

Rank, Otto, 1884-1939.
Truth and reality.
(The Norton Library)
Translation of Wahrheit und Wirklichkeit.
1. Will.   2. Psychoanalysis.   3. Psychology,
Pathological.   4. Psychiatry and religion.
I. Title.
BF613.R313   1978   150'.19'5   78-15067
ISBN 0-393-00899-1

1 2 3 4 5 6 7 8 9 0

CONTENTS

TRANSLATOR'S PREFACE

Truth and Reality is the third volume of Rank's "Grundzüge einer genetischen Psychologie auf Grund der Psychoanalyse der Ichstruktur" (Outlines of a Genetic Psychology on the basis of the Psychoanalysis of the Ego Structure). The first volume, published in 1927, is concerned with the biological development of the ego, including the genesis of genitality, the origin of guilt feeling, and the genesis of the object relation, and discusses the psychic mechanisms such as projection, identification, and denial, an important concept which Rank introduces as more basic than repression. It has never been published in English but was delivered in lecture form under the auspices of the New York School of Social Work in 1926, before it appeared in German.

Volume Two, "Gestaltung und Ausdruck der Persönlichkeit" (The Development of Personality), published in 1928, goes beyond the biological level to the essentially human development of man as an emotional, social and ethical being. It contains discussions of character formation as contrasted with something we call personality, the development of the emotional life, education, social adaptation, creativity, and the helping function. Like the first volume, this book also was presented first in the United States as a lecture course for the New York School of Social Work and for the Pennsylvania School of Social Work in 1927, although it has not appeared in an English translation.

"Truth and Reality," the third volume, like the other two, was offered first in English in lecture form, in this case for the Pennsylvania School of Social Work alone, just before its publication in German in 1929. While it forms the conclusion of the two volumes just described, it presents in clear, integrated form an original point of view representing Rank's unique contribution to psychology and philosophy, which had not come through into full consciousness until this final book was written. Although "The Trauma of Birth," published in German in 1924, marks the

beginning of Rank's development beyond Freudian psychoanalysis, the first two volumes of "Genetische Psychologie," while they
differ radically from the orthodox psychoanalytic approach, are
not yet clearly differentiated from Freudian psychology. Before
the third volume was written Rank had found the key to his own
theoretical organization in a sudden realization of the role of the
will in the analytic situation.

Under the illumination of that discovery he wrote simultaneously the second volume of his "Technik der Psychoanalyse" [1] showing the relation of will to the therapeutic process and
repudiating completely the Freudian psychoanalytic method,
and this third volume of "Genetische Psychologie," "Truth and
Reality," in which he develops the psychological and philosophic
implications underlying his new vision of the therapeutic process.

In "Truth and Reality" Rank offers not one more psychology
of the individual in the interest of therapy, but a philosophy of
man's willing, an historical sketch of the evolution of will itself
with its inexhaustible creativity, its dynamic of projection and
denial and its ever increasing burden of fear and guilt.

J.T.

Philadelphia
December 1935

---

[1] This volume appears as Part One of "Will Therapy."

TRUTH AND REALITY

A LIFE HISTORY OF THE HUMAN WILL

―――――――――

JESUS. *I am come to bear witness unto the truth.*

PILATE: *What is truth?*

I

THE BIRTH OF INDIVIDUALITY

> "The most important event in the life of a
> man is the moment when he becomes con-
> scious of his own ego."   —TOLSTOI

THE lines of thought comprehended in this book constitute a
preliminary statement of the final working out of a concept of
the psychic which I had anticipated in the work of my youth
"Der Künstler" [1] (1905) almost a quarter of a century ago.[2]
The consequent building up and shaping of this early conception led me gradually to a "genetic" and "constructive" psychology which, on the basis of practical analytic experiences, has
finally crystallized into a will psychology. This approach threw
such meaningful light upon the psychological foundation of
epistemology and ethics that it led me ultimately to a philosophy of the psychic which I now attempt to outline in the
following chapters. The practical, therapeutic aspect of the will
psychology I developed in the second part of my "Technique
of Psychoanalysis" which was published simultaneously.[3]

While at first I was completely under the influence of Freudian
realism and tried to express my conception of the creative man,
the artist, in the biological-mechanistic terms of Freud's natural

[1] "Der Künstler. Ansätze zu einer Sexualpsychologie." Hugo Heller, Vienna
and Leipzig 1907. Second and third editions the same 1918. "Der Künstler und
andere Beiträge zur Psychoanalyse des dichterischen Schaffens." Fourth en-
larged edition. International Psychoanalytic Press, Leipzig, Vienna, Zurich
1925 (Imago-Bücher I).
[2] *Translator's Note:* The German word "seelisch" has no exact equivalent in
English. I have used "psychic" in lieu of something better, but it does not
carry satisfactorily the reference to the concept of the soul in primitive
cultures to which Rank relates modern psychology in his book "Seelenglaube
und Psychologie."
[3] "Technik der Psychoanalyse, II. Die analytische Reaktion in ihren kon-
struktiven Elementen." F. Deuticke, Leipzig and Vienna, 1928. English translation, "Will Therapy," Book I. Alfred A. Knopf, 1936.

1

science ideology, on the basis of my own experience, I have since been enabled to formulate these common human problems in a common human language as well. "The Trauma of Birth," [1] a book written in 1923, marks the decisive turning point in this development. There I compared to the creative drive of the individual as treated in "Der Künstler," the creation of the individual himself, not merely physically, but also psychically in the sense of the "rebirth experience," which I understood psychologically as the actual creative act of the human being. For in this act the psychic ego is born out of the biological corporeal ego and the human being becomes at once creator and creature or actually moves from creature to creator, in the ideal case, creator of himself, his own personality.

This conception of the birth of individuality from the self as a consequent psychological carrying out of the original trauma of birth from the mother, leads also to another kind of methodology of treatment and presentation. While in "The Trauma of Birth" I proceeded from a concrete experience in the analytic situation and its new interpretation, and as in "Der Künstler" strove to broaden it into the universally human and cultural, my present conception just reversed is based on the universally human—yes, if you will, on the cosmic idea of soul. and seeks to assemble all its expressions in the focal point of the separate individuality. It has to do neither with a leading back of the general, the supra-individual, to the concrete and personal, nor with a wishing to explain the one from the other. Although this may often be the appearance, yes, at times may even underlie it, yet this is not the object of this presentation which rather sets for itself the goal of viewing the two worlds of macrocosm and microcosm as parallel, and only as far as possible, pointing out their inter-dependence and their reactions upon one another. In this attempt, excursions into the history of culture are naturally unavoidable, in order at least to note the great counterpart of the individual in a few of its typical forms.

[1] "Das Trauma der Geburt und seine Bedeutung für die Psychoanalyse." International Psychoanalytic Press, Leipzig, Vienna, Zurich, 1924 (Internationale Psychoanalytische Bibliothek XIV). French translation in the "Bibliothèque Scientifique," Payot, Paris, 1928. English translation in "International Library of Psychology, Philosophy and Scientific Method," London 1928, Kegan Paul, Trench, Trubner & Co., Ltd.

The main task, however, as indicated in "Genetische Psychologie" continues to be the presentation of the chief actor and at the same time chief onlooker, the individual ego, in this, his dual role. This involves not only the duality of actor and self-observer, but has yet another meaning, in that, for civilized man, the milieu is no longer the natural reality, the opposing force of an external world, but an artistic reality, created by himself which we, in its outer as in its inner aspects, designate as civilization. In this sense civilized man, even if he fights the outside world, is no longer opposed to a natural enemy but at bottom to himself, to his own creation, as he finds himself mirrored, particularly in manners and customs, morality and conventions, social and cultural institutions. The phenomenon thus described is of fundamental meaning for the understanding of the human being's relation to the outer world as well as to his fellow man. For while Freud's reality psychology emphasized essentially the influence of outer factors, of the milieu, upon the development of the individual and the formation of his character, even in "Der Künstler" I opposed to this biological principle, the spiritual principle which alone is meaningful in the development of the essentially human. This is based essentially on the conception that the inner world, taken in from the outside by means of identification has become in the course of time an independent power, which in its turn by way of projection, so influences and seeks to alter the external, that its correspondence to the inner is even more close. This relation to outer reality I designate as creation in contrast to adaptation, and comprehend as will phenomena. The indication of its psychological determinants and dynamic factors in terms of this will psychology, forms the main content of the following chapters.

This conception of the influencing and transforming of the milieu by the individual allows for the inclusion of the creative, the artist type, for whom there is no place in Freud's world picture where all individual expressions are explained as reactions to social influences or as biological instincts and therewith are reduced to something outside the individual. For with Freud the individual in the nucleus of his being (the so-called "id") is subject to the great natural laws, under the guise of the "repetition compulsion," while personality consists of the layers of identifications which form the basis of the parental super-ego. This perhaps may account for the great mass, the average, although even here it can be true only roughly, but it can never explain the creative type nor the so-called "neurotic," who represents the artist's miscarried counterpart. In this cursory survey I should like to characterize the creative type, in a preliminary way only, in this regard, that he is able, in a way soon to be described more closely, to create voluntarily from the impulsive elements and moreover to develop his standards beyond the identifications of the super-ego morality to an ideal formation which consciously guides and rules this creative will in terms of the personality. The essential point in this process is the fact that he evolves his ego ideal from himself, not merely on the ground of given but also of self-chosen factors which he strives after consciously.

As a result the ego, instead of being caught between the two powerful forces of fate, the inner id and the externally derived super-ego, develops and expresses itself creatively. The Freudian ego driven by the libidinal id and restrained by parental morality, becomes almost a nonentity, a helpless tool for which there remains no autonomous function, certainly not willing whether this be creative or only a simple goal conscious striving. In my view the ego is much more than a mere show place for the standing conflict between two great forces. Not only is the individual ego naturally the carrier of higher goals, even when they are built on external identifications, it is also the temporal representative of the cosmic primal force no matter whether one calls it sexuality, libido, or id. The ego accordingly is strong just in the degree to which it *is* the representative of this primal force and the strength of this force represented in the individual we call the will. This will becomes creative, when it carries itself on through the ego into the super-ego and there leads to ideal formations of its own, which, if you will, in the last analysis arise from the id, at all events not from without. On this account, the creative man of every type has a much stronger ego than the average man, as we see not only in genius but also in the neurotic, whose convulsed hypertrophied ego is just what creates the neurosis, psychologically a creative achievement just as much as any other. The creative type, whose denial we see in the inferior neurotic is

4

therefore not only characterized by a stronger impulse life, but also by a wholly special utilization of it, the most important aspect of which I consider the ideal formation from the own self (i. e. on the basis of the own impulsive make-up) whose "negative" we have to recognize in the neurotic symptom formation. However, while the neurotic so strengthens his repressions against his stronger than average impulsive self, that they finally make him completely incapable of willing and acting, in the creative man there occurs a qualitatively different impulse displacement, which manifests itself psychologically as ideal formation with simultaneous expression in conscious creative activity of will. Such a conception makes creative power and creative accomplishment comprehensible for the first time, rather than the insipid and impotent concept of sublimation, which prolongs a shadowy existence in psychoanalysis. From this viewpoint one could say that with human beings sometimes even impulsive expressions are only a weaker, less satisfactory substitute for that which the creative power of will would like. Therefore, as it were, not only the phantasy-produced substitute for unattained reality, but even the reality which is attainable, is only a weaker substitute for the inexhaustible willing.

The psychological understanding of the creative type and of its miscarriage in the neurotic, teaches us therefore to value the ego, not only as a wrestling ground of (id) impulses and (superego) repressions, but also as conscious bearer of a striving force, that is, as the autonomous representative of the will and ethical obligation in terms of a self constituted ideal. Freud's original wish fulfilment theory lay much nearer to this recognition than his later doctrine of instincts, which actually only represented a biologizing of the unconscious wishes. We easily recognize in the Freudian wish the old will of the academic psychologists, although in the romantic guise of natural philosophy, while the wish, as I first explained it in "Der Künstler," actually corresponds to an impulse tendency which later was ascribed to the supra-individual id. But the conscious wish fulfilment tendency of the ego, for the designation of which the suitable word "will" exists, extends (as Freud himself finally had to perceive in "The Ego and Id") much further than he was willing to admit, while the instinctual impulse tendency in men is less extensive than he originally thought, since it is repressed by the powerful super-ego factors for Freud and, for me, in addition, is molded by the self-created ideal formation. Also this fact appears clearly in the dream phenomenon in which Freud has seen the wish fulfilment tendency, since the conscious wishes of the day are often strong enough to put through their fulfilment in dreams while the ostensibly stronger unconscious wishes (the impulse drives) are almost regularly blocked by the ethical repressions, still watchful even in sleep (Freud's censor). All these facts and considerations would have been able to save psychoanalysis from an over-valuation of the power of the unconscious impulsive life in men, and from the under-valuation of his conscious willing ego, if a kind of psychic compulsion, which reaches far beyond the personal psychology of its creator, had not, of necessity, blocked it. Before we seek the source and nature of this compulsion, I should like to justify here briefly by way of introduction what causes me to speak of a compulsion. The whole of psychoanalysis in its theoretical and practical aspects is actually an unparalleled glorification of consciousness and its power as I have already observed in "Der Künstler," while Freud himself designates his theory as a psychology of the unconscious and as such wishes it to be understood. It certainly is that, too, but the more it became a doctrine of the unconscious, the less it remained psychology. As a theory of the unconscious it became a biological foundation of psychology as which I also tried to present it in "Der Künstler." In its mechanisms of super-ego formation it gives on the other hand a foundation of characterology. The actual field of psychology, the conscious ego, with its willing, its sense of duty, and its feeling, psychoanalysis has treated very like a step-child because it has placed the ego almost entirely under the guardianship of extra-individual factors, of the id and the super-ego, at least as far as theory is concerned. In practice, however, psychoanalysis represents, as has already been said, a glorification of the power of consciousness; in its therapeutic meaning, according to which neurosis is cured by making conscious the unconscious motive underlying it, in its cultural significance as a tremendous broadening of consciousness in the development of humanity, as I represented it in "Der Künstler," and finally in its scientific meaning, as the recognition and knowledge of a part of the unconscious in nature.

Before we can investigate how such a contradiction could arise between theory formation, the facts on which it rests, and the conclusions to which it leads, we must review the factors which, according to our viewpoint, psychoanalysis has undervalued. At first we said it was the significance of the inner, independently of the outer factors, then the significance of the creative will, and finally the meaning of a conscious sense of duty. We recognize now that these factors belong together intimately and condition one another, yes, in a certain sense, represent one and the same thing. We started from the "inner" which originally was an "outer," but became inner, and as its representative we accept the super-ego in the Freudian sense, that is, as far as it is built up on identifications. If we add to this "outer" also the id which is in a certain sense supra-individual because generic, that which Jung designates in the racial sense as collective unconscious, there remains left over as the actual own "inner" of the individual, his ego, which we have distinguished as bearer of the creative will, or generally speaking, of the conscious personality. If we have once acknowledged its power—and psychoanalysis, as already said, had recognized but denied it—there appear as a result further interesting perspectives which the old academic psychology in spite of its recognition of the meaning of conscious willing, could not let itself dream of because it lacked the dynamic viewpoint which psychoanalysis, it is true, conceived purely on the level of biological instinct while we approach it rather from the basis of the individual creative.

First of all, there is the possibility of the creative reaction of this strengthened willing ego upon the overcome instinctual id; on the other hand, there follows therefrom the already noted influencing of the super-ego formation through the self-constructed ideal. The first effect leads us into the most important but also the darkest field of all psychology, namely, the emotional life, while the effect of the willing ego, on the other side, comprehends all actual sublimation phenomena, therefore the spiritual, in the broadest sense. In a word we encounter here for the first time the actual ground of psychology, the realm of willing and ethics in the purely psychic, not in the biological or moral sense, therefore not in terms of any supra-individual force, but of freedom as Kant understood it metaphysically, that is, beyond external influences. Psychoanalysis has scarcely approached the problem of the emotional life because the "unconscious" feelings which it accepted corresponding to the "unconscious" wishes were not so easily reducible to instinctive life as the latter. In want of a better explanation, one could perhaps allow the assumption to serve that the affects correspond to such unconscious feelings but the whole sphere of human emotions, important as they are, with their finely graded scale is as undeniably a phenomenon of consciousness, as the whole man himself. One can better accept from this standpoint the Freudian explanation of consciousness as a "sense organ for the perception of psychic qualities" in the genetic sense. Probably consciousness even earlier was entirely a sense organ for the perception of external qualities (sensation psychology) which it still is today also; later was added the function of the perception of inner qualities and a further developmental level of consciousness was that of an independent and spontaneous organ for partial ruling of the outer as of the inner world. Finally, consciousness became an instrument of observation and knowledge of itself (self-consciousness) and as such again it has reached in psychoanalysis and the will psychology which I built further upon it, a peak of development and self-knowledge. The individual ego frees itself therefore always more and more with the weapon of increased power of consciousness, not only from the rule of environmental natural forces, but also from the biological reproduction compulsion of the overcome id; it influences thereby also more and more positively the super-ego development in terms of the self-constructed ideal formation and finally in a creative sense the outer world, whose transformation through men on its side again reacts upon the ego and its inner development.

Thus we are finally led back again from the problem of will to the problem of consciousness and this all the more, the more psychological we remain. For however fundamental and important the will—whatever one may understand by that—for all stimulation of the individual to acting, feeling and thinking, finally we can only comprehend all these phenomena in and through consciousness. In this deeper sense psychology can of necessity be nothing other than a psychology of consciousness; yes, even more, a psychology of consciousness in its various aspects and phases of development. We shall examine later this relativity, not only of all conscious human knowledge, but of all phenomena of consciousness itself. First of all we face the whole problem of psychology, namely, that we become aware of the actual driving factors in our psychic life always only through the medium of consciousness, but that this consciousness itself is nothing firm, constant, or unalterable. There results from this situation a series of difficulties without knowledge of which every psychology is impossible, since the understanding of these contradictions forms the very warp and woof of phychology as such. These difficulties are: first, that we, as said, are aware of the will phenomena only through the medium of consciousness; second, that this conscious self offers us no fixed standpoint for observation of these phenomena, but itself ceaselessly alters, displaces and broadens them. This leads to the third and perhaps most important point, namely, that we can observe these fluctuating phenomena of consciousness itself only through a kind of super-consciousness which we call self-consciousness.

The difficulties are complicated still more seriously when we take into consideration the fact that consciousness itself and its development are determined essentially by will phenomena or at least are influenced in far reaching fashion. We can hardly do justice to this highly complicated state of affairs when we say that a constant interpretation and reinterpretation takes place from both sides. Consciousness is constantly interpreted by will and the various levels of will, yes, consciousness originally is itself probably a will phenomenon; that is, consciousness was an instrument for the fulfilment of will before it advanced to the will controlling power of self-consciousness and finally of analytic hyperconsciousness, which on its side again interprets will and will phenomena continuously in order to make it useful for its momentary interests. If we actually want to pursue psychology we must protect ourselves from extending further this constantly reciprocal process of interpretation by any kind of theory formation. Theory formation of every kind is then only

9

an attempt to oppose to the manifold spontaneous attempts at interpretation by will and consciousness a single interpretation as constant, lasting, true. This, however, on the basis of the considerations just presented, is exactly anti-psychological, since the essence of psychic processes consists in change and in the variability of the possibilities of interpretation. The compulsion to theory formation corresponds then to a longing after a firm hold, after something constant, at rest, in the flight of psychic events. Is there perhaps some way out, which might free us from this external compulsion to interpretation or at least let us rest a moment beyond it? Certainly it is not the way of historical or genetic analysis. For aside from the fact that even the final elements to which we can arrive by this path still represent phenomena of interpretation, it is also unavoidable that on the uninterrupted analytic path to these elements we should fall upon the interpretation compulsion of consciousness and of the will also. There remains therewith psychologically no other recourse than just the recognition of this condition and perhaps also an attempt to understand why it must be so. This would be the purely psychological problem, beyond which there begins again the kind of interpretation which we designate as knowledge in the broadest sense of the word. This knowledge, however, is not an interpretative understanding, but an immediate experiencing, therefore a form of the creative, perhaps the highest form of which man is capable, certainly the most dangerous form, because it can finally lead to pain, if it opposes itself to living inhibitingly, instead of confirming it pleasurably. We shall treat in the following chapters this contrast between knowing and experiencing which culminates finally in the problem of "truth or reality" in order eventually to recognize in the opposition of the most longed for psychic states of happiness and salvation, the double role of consciousness or of conscious knowing, as the source of all pleasure but also of all suffering.

Here I should like to go further by way of introduction as far as the location of the problem itself is concerned, and estimate the value of knowledge for the understanding of our own soul life. We sought before for a way out from the contradictory interpretative compulsion, in which will excites consciousness and consciousness excites will. It is that kind of knowledge which one can best designate as philosophic because at least its tendency is directed not upon this or that content but upon the existence of the phenomena themselves. The philosopher creates, as little as the artist or the religious believer, merely from his own personality. What manifests itself in all of them, although in different form, is at once something supra-individual, natural, cosmic, which accordingly and to this extent also has value somehow for all humanity. At all events here we run against the problem of form, which is just the essential thing psychologically. But in the creative individual, in genius, there is manifested, becomes more or less conscious, not only a bit of the primal, but just as much the individual, the personal. How far and to what extent the knowledge is universally valid depends entirely on the relation of these two elements in this mixture and their effect on each other. At all events, the individual is liable to the danger, or at least the attempt, of again interpreting the universal which becomes conscious of itself in him in terms of his individual personal development, that is, speaking psychologically, of representing it as an expression of his will and not of a supra-individual force (compulsion). This is the psychology of the world view which in contrast to theory building, as we have previously characterized it, as flight from the interpretative doubt, represents an immediate creative experience not only of the individual himself, but of the cosmos manifested in him.

Again here, on the highest peak of the human elevation of consciousness and its creative expression, we run upon the same basic conflict of will and compulsion which goes through the whole development of man and the process of becoming conscious. In the creative individual this conflict is manifest only at times, and we can best describe it thus, that nature becomes even more conscious of herself in a man who at the same time with the increasing knowledge of himself which we designate as individualization, tries always to free himself further from the primitive. It has to do, therefore, with a conflictual separation of the individual from the mass, undertaken and continued at every step of development into the new, and this I should like to designate as the never completed birth of individuality. For the whole consequence of evolution from blind impulse through conscious

11

will to self conscious knowledge, seems still somehow to correspond to a continued result of births, rebirths and new births, which reach from the birth of the child from the mother, beyond the birth of the individual from the mass, to the birth of the creative work from the individual and finally to the birth of knowledge from the work. In this sense, the contrast of will and consciousness as we have recognized it as the psychological problem par excellence, somehow corresponds to the biological contrast of procreation and birth. At all events we find in all these phenomena, even at the highest spiritual peak, the struggle and pain of birth, the separation out of the universal, with the pleasure and bliss of procreation, the creation of an own individual cosmos, whether it be now physically our own child, creatively our own work or spiritually our own self. At bottom it is and remains our own act of will, which we oppose to the outer force of reality as the inner pressure after truth.

II

WILL AND FORCE

> "Man is fearful of things which cannot
> hurt him and he knows it; and he longs for
> things which can be of no good to him and
> he knows it; but in truth it is something in
> man himself of which he is afraid and it is
> something in man himself for which he
> longs." —RABBI NACHMAN

MY RE-INTRODUCTION of the will concept into psychology solves
a succession of problems in such a simple and satisfying way that
it may seem to some a deus ex machina. But I know too well that
I have not brought it in as such; on the contrary that I have
busied myself long and intensively in the attempt to solve certain
problems which psychoanalysis had brought up anew without
coming to a satisfactory solution. Only after a struggle against
prejudices of every kind did the acceptance of will as a psychological factor of the first rank seem unavoidable but soon also
became a matter of course, so much a matter of course that I
had to say to myself that only a tremendous resistance could
have hindered the complete recognition and evaluation of will
as a great psychic power.

Thus the problem soon presented itself to me as a universal
one, going far beyond the critique of psychoanalysis. Why must
will be denied if it actually plays so great a role in reality, or to
formulate it in anticipation, why is the will valued as bad, evil,
reprehensible, unwelcome, when it is the power which consciously
and positively, yes even creatively, forms both the self and the
environment? If one puts the problem thus, then one sees at the
same time that this apparently necessary contradiction is not
only the basic problem of all psychology, but lies at the root of
all religious dogma as well as of all philosophic speculation. In
a word, not only all religion and philosophy are avowedly moral-

13

istic but psychology was also and must continue to be, as long as it cannot place itself beyond this will problem and thus be able to solve it. Religion and philosophy are, as we know, highly valued because of their moralistic tendencies and their ethical content while it is the pride of psychologists to deny this weakness in their science. Certainly psychology should not be moralistic, but it was necessarily so as long and as far as it busied itself with the content of soul life which is saturated and pierced through and through with moralistic principles. To an unusual degree this is true for therapeutically oriented psychoanalysis and that constitutes in my mind its greatest advantage as an educational method. As psychology it has been obliged in its theory formation to justify this moral-pedagogic character in part and in part to deny it. However anti-moralistic psychoanalysis may seem, at bottom for Freud, will—or whatever he understands by that term—is exactly as "bad" as for the Old Testament man or the Buddhist or the Christian, exactly as reprehensible as it still is for Schopenhauer or other philosophers who played reason against it.

The problem therefore is not peculiarly psychoanalytic, not even purely psychological, but cultural and human. Its solution depends upon one single point. The conception of will as evil, its condemnation or justification, is the basic psychological fact which we must understand and explain instead of criticizing it or taking it as presupposition or finally as a primary phenomenon as psychoanalysis has done in the concept of guilt. That is the point at which real psychology begins. That psychoanalysis could not go on beyond this point is understandable from its nature as a therapeutic method. Psychoanalysis began as therapy, its knowledge comes from that source and psychotherapy according to its nature must be oriented morally or at least normatively. Whether it has to do with the medical concept of normality or with the social concept of adaptation, therapy can never be without prejudice for it sets out from the standpoint that something should be otherwise than it is, no matter how one may formulate it. Psychology, on the contrary, should describe what it is, how it is, and, where possible, explain why it must be so. These two diametrically opposed principles, Janus-headed psychoanalysis has necessarily mixed up and the lack of insight into this condition as well as a later denial has finally led to such confusion that now therapy is psychologically oriented and theory moralistically so instead of the reverse.

A closer interpretation of this paradoxical state of affairs will best lead into the understanding of the will problem underlying it. The psychoanalytic patient seemed in the beginning to suffer from repression of impulse, from inhibitions; evidently because he denied impulse as bad, as unethical. One can quite well imagine therapy resulting when an authority (doctor or priest) or a loving person permits the individual this impulse satisfaction; in other words says to him, "It is not bad as you assert, but good (necessary, beautiful, etc.)." This kind of therapy has always existed and still does today, in religion, in art, and in love. Also psychoanalysis began with it and essentially has always remained with it. First it operated directly, as Freud encouraged his patients to a normal sexual relation, that is, psychologically speaking, permitted it. But even in all the complicated outgrowths of psychoanalytic therapy and theory this one justification tendency still remains the actually effective therapeutic agent. Only now they say, "your evil wishes"—as prototypes of which Œdipus and castration wishes, the worst that man can wish, are brought forth—"are not evil, or at least you are not responsible for them for they are universal." That is not only correct but is often therapeutically effective especially with trusting natures, not in the ironical but in the psychological sense of the word, with men who always seek some kind of excuse for their willing and find it now in the id instead of in God. But as men have seen through the so-called priestly deception, which actually is a self-deception, so they finally see through every kind of therapeutic self-deception and it is just that from which they suffer, just that which forms the very root of the neurosis. When I say "see through," I do not mean necessarily consciously, but guilt feeling, which humanity perceives always and ever increasingly in spite of this apparent absence of responsibility, is the best proof of what this kind of therapy denies today, in a certain sense has always denied, and to that extent has worked only partially.

In what I have already described in "Der Künstler" as the spontaneous therapies of human kind, religion, art, philosophy, this form of consolation works, partly because of their universality, partly because in them man accuses himself of this evil will that he would like to deny. In ritual, in artistic satisfaction, in teaching, man is unburdened and comforted through the others, the priests, the artists, the wise. But in the content of these therapeutic systems, accusation and punishment dominate as religious humility, resignation, as tragic guilt and sin, and as justification in terms of the ethical reaction formation. In a word, in all these projections of the great will conflict, man confesses in one or another way that he is himself sinful, guilty, bad. Exactly the same process of justification and self accusation we see unroll itself in psychoanalysis only here it appears in the therapeutic and psychological terminology of our natural science age, although it seems unavoidable to bring in the contentually richer ideas and symbols of earlier systems. In its technique, psychoanalysis is exactly as much a matter of consolation and justification as therapy must be according to its nature. That is, it quiets man concerning his badness, since it says to him that all others are thus also and that it lies grounded in human nature. Therefore psychoanalysis in the content of its system, of its theory, must count exactly as all the former justification attempts of humanity. In psychoanalytic theory, instinct is evil, bad, reprehensible; the individual is small and insignificant, a play-ball of the id and the super-ego; guilt feeling is and remains a final insoluble fact.

Hence it comes about that psychoanalytic theory represents the necessary opposite to the therapy, as the religious system or church dogma represents the necessary opposite to ritualistic practice, the ritual of atonement. It is a completion just as the creative work of the individual represents a completion and not merely an expression of actual experience. It follows that psychoanalysis cannot be an independent unprejudiced psychology but must be the necessary balance to its therapeutic practice, often enough its willing servant.

It is still psychology, even so, but it becomes the psychology of the therapist, who needs such a theory for the justification of his practice and simultaneously for the denial of his moral-pedagogical attitude. In this sense, however, this very attitude itself again becomes the object of psychology which asks further why every kind of therapist needs a justification at all and why just this one? The objection that psychoanalytic theory is founded on the experiences of the practice of therapy and that just this constitutes its value, especially its scientific value is not entirely sound. Psychoanalytic theory is founded on one single experience, the fact of the analytic situation, which however is an essentially therapeutic one, that is, rests on the relation of the patient to the doctor. As the patient represents the object, could one expect to obtain even in the summation of his various experiences, a universal human psychology? It would represent only the psychology of a part of humanity, let us say even of the majority, namely those in need of help. The psychology of the helper, of the therapist, would remain and this side of human nature is at least just as important.

My contention goes far beyond this conclusion in maintaining that psychoanalysis betrays much more of the psychology of the therapist, of the helper, of the active willing person, only it represents it as the psychology of the patient, the seeker for help, the willness. This is not to deny the psychological value of psychoanalysis in which as I believe, we can study the fundamental problems of human soul life as never before and nowhere else, only we must first agree on certain basic questions upon whose clarification our fruitful utilization of psychoanalysis depends. In a word, the psychology of the normal man, the average type given us by psychoanalysis is in reality the psychology of the creative man, not only of Freud, as Michaelis has shown beautifully in the single case,[1] but of the type. It unveils to us the psychology of the strong man of will, who while almost God himself and creator of men in his practice, in his theory must deny his godlikeness with all its characteristics and represent himself as a small, weak, helpless creature, a person actually seeking help and comfort.

Although enough human tragedy lies in this apparently unavoidable fate of the creative type, the denial continued into the work, the philosophy, darkens its noble aspect. For the work born out of this superhuman internal struggle to represent an

[1] Edgar Michaelis: "Die Menschheitsproblematik der Freudschen Psychoanalyse. Urbild und Maske. Eine grundsätzliche Untersuchung zur neueren Seelenforschung." Leipzig 1925.

infallible revelation of the latest universally valid psychological truth may be comprehensible as a reaction against the content of the system, but brings so many trifling features into the picture of the personality as well that the tragedy almost turns into a farce. Nietzsche, who experienced thoroughly the whole tragedy of the creative man and admitted in his "amor fati" the willingness to pay for it, is in my opinion the first and has been up to now the only psychologist. He was at all events the first who recognized the "moral" danger in every philosophizing and psychologizing and sought to avoid it. He would have succeeded still better, that is at a lesser cost, if he had recognized the necessity of the "moral" in all psychologizing (including the therapeutic) instead of analyzing the philosophers from that viewpoint in so masterly a way. At any rate he recognized the problem and was right to see in it a danger for himself first of all, although correctly understood it is not the common danger he made it. In this sense he is at all events much less philosopher, that is, moralist, than Freud for example and accordingly also much more a psychologist than he. Certainly his freedom from office and calling which he had to buy so dearly had much to do with it. In no case, however, was he a therapist who needed a psychological justification, no, not even a patient, a seeker for help, in spite of all his illnesses. He was himself, which is the first requirement for a psychologist, and therefore he was also the first and only one who could affirm the evil will, who even glorified it. That was his psychological product for which he paid not with system building and scientific rationalization, but with personal suffering, with his own experience.

Nietzsche's contribution, therefore, based on Schopenhauer's important discovery of will, is the separation of the will from the guilt problem (the moral). He has not completely solved the problem, could not solve it, because for its solution the analytic experience was necessary. By which I mean not so much the experiences of the analyst through the patient, but also and much more the experience of humanity with psychoanalysis. As Nietzsche's will affirmation represents a reaction to the will denial of the Schopenhauerian system, so Freud's theory is again to be understood as a throwback from Nietzsche's attitude to an almost Schopenhauerian pessimism and nihilism. I do not doubt that my will psychology which has arisen from personal experiences, represents in its turn a reaction against Freud's "making evil" of the will; I shall show further that the whole history of mankind in the individual himself and in the race represents just such a sequence of will action and reaction, of affirmation and denial. I shall then show also that in the historical developmental process of this will conflict, as in its individual manifestations we have to do not merely with a repetition in the sense of the Freudian fatalism but that a continuous evolution can be traced in terms of the broadening of consciousness and the development of self-consciousness. For as little as Freud's theory is a "repetition" of the closely related one of Schopenhauer, so little has my will psychology to do with Nietzsche's "will to power," with which Nietzsche has again finally smuggled evaluation into psychology. With this comparison I mean only to point to a common psychological aspect of experience, which necessarily conditions these reactions, and which we intend to make the object of our investigation.

The will in itself is not as "evil" as the Jew-hating Schopenhauer believes along with the Old Testament, nor as "good" as the sick Nietzsche would like to see it in his glorification. It exists as a psychological fact and is the real problem of psychology, first as to its origin, how it has evolved in man, and second why we must condemn it as "bad" or justify it as "good," instead of recognizing and affirming it as necessary. The epistemological question, whence it comes, what it means psychologically, will throw a light upon the ethical question of condemnation or justification in the answering of which, however, we must guard against bringing in moralistic evaluations before we have recognized their psychological source. Which is to say also that we must guard against bringing therapeutic viewpoints into psychology with Freud, or pedagogical aims with Adler, or ethical values with Jung, for at bottom they all involve one and the same cardinal error. That the will must be justified in therapy, we already know, yes, even the patient is caught in the denial of it, that is in guilt feeling, and his seeking for help is just an expression of this will conflict. That the will in pedagogy

19

is reprehensible, goes without saying, for pedagogy is obviously a breaking of the will as ethics is a will limitation and therapy will justification.

If I said we must guard ourselves against bringing in therapeutic elements, that is, moral evaluations into psychology, then I must elucidate this further before I go into a sketch of a philosophy of the psychic (seelisch). Although my will psychology has resulted not wholly from analytic experience, but also represents the result of my philosophic, pedagogic, religious and cultural studies, still I will not deny that it was essentially analytic practice that crystallized for me all of these various materials, differing in kind and value, into a psychological experience. I must present these analytic experiences elsewhere not only from lack of space but also on objective grounds in order to exclude as much as possible a mixture of the two viewpoints since they correspond to two different world views. But this external separation would not necessarily guarantee an inner separation if I had not at the same time in my analytic work struggled through to a technique which tries to avoid the therapeutic in the moral pedagogical sense. What, you will probably ask, is this new method and what does it aim at if not re-education since any cure for mental suffering is excluded anyway?[1] To say it in one word, the aim is self development; that is, the person is to develop himself into that which he is and not as in education and even in analytic therapy to be made into a good citizen, who accepts the general ideals without contradiction and has no will of his own. This, as Keyserling[2] recently noted pertinently, is the confessed purpose of Adler's leveling pedagogical cure and as Prinzhorn[3] has seen, the unconfessed but clear purpose of Freudian psychoanalysis which purports to be revolutionary but is really conservative. If one understood the will psychology only a little, one must at least know that this conservatism is the best method of breeding revolutionary, willful men who for the most part are driven into

[1] See the observations on "Leiden und Helfen" in Part II of my "Genetische Psychologie."

[2] "Vom falschen Gemeinschaftsideal" (Der Weg zur Vollendung, 14 Heft, 1927).

[3] Hans Prinzhorn: "Leib-Seele—Einheit." Ein Kernproblem der neuen Psychologie, 1927.

the neurosis by the oppressive majority when they want to express their wills. No, the man who suffers from pedagogical, social and ethical repression of will, must again learn to will, and not to force on him an alien will is on the other hand the best protection against excesses of will which for the most part only represent reactions. In my view the patient should make himself what he is, should will it and do it himself, without force or justification and without need to shift the responsibility for it.

How I present the method leading to this end and utilize it practically, I will discuss elsewhere. Here it has this value only; to show how and in how far I can apply my practical experiences to the founding of my will psychology justifiably because as a matter of fact they are not therapeutic in the moralistic pedagogical sense but are constructive. Otherwise I should not have succeeded at all in understanding what a tremendous role will psychology plays in general. In the Freudian analysis the patient is measured by a minimum scale, as it were, as perhaps the weak-sighted by the ophthalmologist in order to be brought up to normal vision. This minimum scale consists of the primitive fear pictures of the Œdipus and castration complexes together with all related sadistic, cannibalistic and narcissistic tendencies. Measured by these the modern civilized man certainly feels himself better than the more evil primitive, at all events not worse, and thus we get the basis for the therapeutic justification. Please do not misunderstand me. I am not making fun of this, any more than of the necessary profession of the ophthalmologist or the normal vision of my chauffeur. But if, for example, a weak visioned painter can create better pictures when he works without glasses, it would be folly to educate him to the wearing of spectacles because he then would see the same as his neighbor the banker. It is just as foolish to educate a man who is inhibited in his self-development by the norm of the Œdipus complex, which he seeks to escape. By this holding up of a mythological decalogue as a confessional mirror one can probably work therapeutically, but one must know what one does, not for the sake of a fanatical sense of honor, but in order to be able to succeed in actuality. However, one must also be ready to admit that the morality lying at the bottom of this therapy is the Jewish-Christian morality which it seeks to conserve, while that part of hu-

21

manity which has already outgrown it includes the main body of
neurotics, whom one can scarcely hope to cure with the morality
from which as a matter of fact they suffer. That, however, is the
therapeutic significance of the Œdipus complex; a kind of
mythologizing of the fourth commandment, which perhaps still
lingers in the Greek Œdipus story but, as I shall show, is certainly not its meaning.

Psychologically the Œdipus complex as I have already indicated in my "Genetische Psychologie" has no other significance
than that of a great—even if not the first—will conflict between
the growing individual and the counter will of a thousand year
old moral code, represented in the parents. Against this itself,
nothing is to be said; it must probably have its value as it has
so long preserved itself and thereby apparently mankind. The
child must subject himself to it, not in order that he should
let his father live and not marry his mother, but that he should
not believe in general that he can do what he wishes, that he
should not even trust himself to will. Also on another ground
than that of the dominance of the strongest must one render
acknowledgment to this old testament moral code against which
perhaps at bottom all hatred of Jews is directed. Apparently we
have to thank the reaction against it for all great revolutionaries
of spirit and deed, who have displaced the old. For on this powerful imprint of centuries the counter will strengthens itself, trains
itself, must first of all seek the most different by-paths and
disguises, in order finally to prevail, and when it has reached this
goal, deny itself in guilt feeling.

Here only a constructive therapy, which must not even be an
individual therapy, can take hold helpfully. I do not mean constructive in the sense of a medically oriented normal therapy as
it is handled in the analytic situation by Freud, who interprets
as resistance the counter will of the patient awakened by the
authoritative pressure of the therapist. Here lies the moralistic
pitfall into which the analyst falls hopelessly when he steps in as
therapist of society and not of the individual. For against this
parent-like representative of the social will is aroused the self
will of the weakest patient although it is interpreted by the
Freudian therapist as resistance on the basis of his own will and
in terms of his own social and moral ideals; that is, as some-

thing which must be overcome or even broken instead of being furthered and developed. Without the understanding and courage of a constructive therapy, individual therapy degenerates into a mass education which is based on the traditional world view and the Jewish-Christian morality. We shall see elsewhere in how far a freeing of will in education, as it is already utilized today in the program of modern pedagogy, works and is justified psychologically. At all events, to correct always seems easier to me than to prevent or to educate, particularly because there is a natural tendency to self healing, yes, even to over-healing (in Ostwald's sense), while the tendency to self education if it exists, at all events is much harder to awaken and to develop, as it presupposes on the part of the individual the acceptance of his own will. This tendency, the constructive technique which I have evolved in individual cases, tries to build up into a principle of individualization, the presentation of which I must postpone to a later time after the fundamental psychological problem of will and force is known and recognized in its universal meaning.

III

KNOWING AND EXPERIENCING

"As the fish does not live outside of the dark abyss,
So man should never strive for knowledge regarding his own essence."
—LAO-TSE

SINCE we have come back to our original point of departure, the overcoming of external force through the inner freedom of will, we have now to indicate in a general way how we conceive the outline of a philosophy of the psychic after this neo-Copernican reversal to conscious will as the central point of psychology, if not of world history. Consciousness, as an instrument of knowledge turned toward the inside seeks truth, that is, inner actuality in contrast to the outer truth of the senses, the so-called "reality." Instinct lifted into the ego sphere by consciousness is the power of will, and at the same time a tamed, directed, controlled instinct, which manifests itself freely within the individual personality, that is, creatively. Indeed it is as free toward the outer as toward the inner. But only the inner effects interest us here, first upon the id, the instinct life itself, and next upon the higher super-ego aspects and ideal formations of the self. Just as the creative will represents the conscious expression of instinct, in a banal sense the act, so emotion represents the conscious awareness of instinct, that is, the emotional tone is an index of the "what" of the will. In both cases, however, it is consciousness which lends to the phenomenon its authentic psychological significance.

The influence of the power of consciousness on the ego-ideal formation has a double effect in the ethical sphere likewise, an active and passive one, corresponding to the act of will and the emotional perception in the purely psychic sphere; active in the creative expression of the momentary ego ideal as it manifests

24

itself in work; passive in the formation of definite ethical, aesthetic, and logical norms for doing and making, without whose concurrence no kind of action is possible. Nay more, these norms modify still further the content of the original pure instinctual drives, which were already modified by consciousness and indeed go beyond content into form, since they prescribe the only possible form in which this particular individual can realize and objectify the content of the momentary instinctual drive. In a word, in the perceptual sphere of emotional life the ego modifies the instincts (lifted into the sphere of will by being made conscious) into definite interests or desires whose carrying over into deed or work again depends on the spiritual forms, if you will, the psychological categories, created from the individual's ego-ideal formation. This is the schema of a constructive will psychology, in the center of which we again place the conscious ego, with its old rights and newly won prerogatives.

From this constructive psychology it is only a step to a widely comprehensive point of view which I designate as a philosophy of the psychic because it includes not only the psychological problem of "Will and Force" but also the epistemological problem of "Truth and Reality," the ethical problem of "Creation and Guilt" and finally, the religious problem of "Happiness and Salvation." And I believe it is impossible to handle or to understand any one without the others. For at the moment when we perceive the mechanism of the instinctive drive set in motion, molded into ethical willing by the conscious ego (and this has been abstracted from a wealth of observation and experience), a reaction results with hitherto incomprehensible inexorableness, a reaction which psychoanalysis has designated as guilt feeling. This guilt feeling in spite of all the efforts of psychoanalysis remains not only an unsolved riddle, but in my opinion has led the whole of psychology astray, including psychoanalysis. For this guilt feeling which seems to enter so inevitably into the functioning of the psychic mechanism like the friction in the operation of a machine, leads to the rationalization of our motives, to the interpretation of our emotions, to the falsifying of truth, and to the doubting of the justification of our will. However, as soon as we restore to the will its psychological rights, the whole of psychology becomes of necessity a psychology of consciousness, which it is anyway according to its nature, and the "psychology of the unconscious" unveils itself to us as one of the numerous attempts of mankind to deny the will in order to evade the conscious responsibility following of necessity therefrom. The unavoidable guilt feeling shows the failure of this attempt, is as it were the "neurotic" throw-back of the denied responsibility. This enthroning of the conscious will upon its natural rights is no backward step from psychoanalytic knowledge, but a necessary step forward and beyond it to include the psychological understanding of the psychoanalytic world view itself.

Freud's presentation of the "Ego and the Id" presents a developmental level of our mental life as it may have existed once and perhaps in the child's development it returns to that level to a certain degree, where the ego, as it were, shyly lifts its head out of the id, perhaps even then against it, and comes upon the moralistic super-ego factors as they are represented by the parent authorities externally. But from this birth hour of the ego from the womb of the id to the self conscious pride—yes, analytic super-pride—of the achieved ego consciousness is a long and highly complicated path which Freud does not follow through, and has not even seen, as he still insists on understanding the modern individual from the earlier level. The conscious ego of the individual since the time of the setting up of father rule, although this still exists formally, has itself become a proud tyrant, who, like Napoleon is not satisfied with the position of a leading general or first consul, nor even with the role of an emperor among kings, but would become ruler of the whole world kingdom. Herein lies the unavoidable tragedy of the ego and from this springs its guilt also. Speaking purely psychologically, as we presented it in our schema of a constructive psychology, the ego had gradually become the conscious interpreter and executor of the impulsive self and as long as it was or could be only that, it found no hindrance in the ethical norms of the ideal ego. Man was one with himself as he had been one with nature before the development of the conscious ego. The inner tragedy, which we designate as conflict, and the guilt necessarily inhering in it, appear only when to the purely interpretative "I will" (which I must do anyway) is added the "It is not so" which denies the necessity.

This goes along with an alteration of consciousness as well as the power of will. Consciousness, which primarily had been only an expression and tool of the will, soon becomes a self dependent power, which can not only support and strengthen the will by rationalization, but also is able to repress it through denial. On the other hand, the will which up to then had been only executive now becomes creative, but at first only negatively so, that is, in the form of a denial. The next step serves to justify and maintain this denial and leads to the positive creation of that which should be, that is, to that which is as the ego wills it in terms of its own ideal formation. Psychologically speaking, this means, as the ego wants the id. I believe, however, that this ego-ideal formation not only works transformingly upon the id, but is itself the consequence of an id already influenced by the will.

Perhaps these last statements of process may seem to many a mere playing with words, an accusation to which most philosophic discussions as well as psychological formulations are easily open. Language, which is the only material of psychological research and philosophic presentation, is rightly famed for a sheer uncreative psychological profundity. Certainly it seems to me that verbal expression itself represents a psychological formulation if not actually an interpretation. Instead of turning to a "philosophy of grammar" to which Freud's opposition of "I and it" would indeed give occasion, we will illustrate the thoughts we have just formulated in psychological terminology with the plastic picture speech of mythical religious symbolism. The nucleus of all mythical religious tradition is the nobility and tragic fall of the hero who comes to grief through his own presumption and the guilt arising therefrom. That is the myth of humanity, ever recurring in the various levels of development involving man in his two aspects as a willing and a self-conscious individual. The hero myth shows man more as willing, the religious myth shows him more as an ethical individual. In relation to the portentous advance of the power of consciousness, the biblical myth of the fall has presented the human tragedy in its noblest form. Man, who advances like God in his omniscience, falls away from nature through consciousness, becomes unfortunate in that he loses his naïve unity with the unconscious, with nature. Here we see for the first time in

27

our presentation, but by no means for the first time in the history of mankind, unconsciousness, oneness with nature, identified with the wholesome, the good, and consciousness with fate.[1] Psychoanalysis notoriously preaches just the opposite, but only in its therapy, while theoretically it must enthrone the unconscious in order to unburden consciousness.

Without going into the broader meaning of the myth of the fall at this point, I should like to illustrate its difference from the hero myth as classic Greece represents it. There man, the hero, appears as creator, as actor, and his likeness to God comes to expression in his deeds, as for example with Prometheus, who, like the Gods, presumes to create men. The biblical myth on the contrary represents this Godlikeness, not on the creative level, but on the level of consciousness, that is, it consists in knowing, in self-consciousness. The contrast between these two myths, the religious and the heroic, signifies not only a contrast between different races, times, and developmental levels, but between two world views, or better said, between two great principles, which we here seek to comprehend as experience and knowledge, living and knowing. The hero myth represents experience (living), the deed, the will, which consciousness could only restrict, as we find it expressed in the Œdipus story [2] but the hero comes to grief and must come to grief in the fact that he cannot know beforehand and does not even want to know so that he can act. The religious myth represents "knowing," the knowledge of God, that is, self knowledge, and here man suffers again in that, knowledge about himself interferes with naïve action, restrains him and torments without affording him the satisfaction and liberation which the deed grants. He cannot accomplish through action any more because he thinks, because he knows too much. Now man longs for naïve unconsciousness as the source of happiness, and curses the knowledge bought so dearly. In the heroic myth the moral runs that with a little insight into pride of will, the fall could have been avoided, which is not correct, but at all events it

[1] See in this connection the literary remains of Alfred Seidel who committed suicide, published by Prinzhorn under this title, "Bewusztsein als Verhängnis," Bonn 1927.

[2] See also "Will Therapy," Book I, chap. v.

represents knowledge as the source of salvation and the strong active will as fate.

Here is shown again the fact that there is no criterion for what is good or bad, as there is no absolute criterion for true or false, since it is one thing at one time, and another at another. The psychological problem which has been raised by this way of understanding myths is in my opinion the basic problem of all psychology which I should like to formulate thus: Why must we always designate one side as bad or false and the other as good or right? This primary psychological problem cannot be answered by saying that we do it because it has been learned from our parents and they again from their parents and so on, back to the original pair. That is the explanation which the Bible gives and Freud also in his primal horde hypothesis. Our individualistic ethics is explicable psychologically but not historically. It is not a cumulative phenomenon of morals piled one upon the other for centuries, nor could it be propagated through centuries if something in the individual himself did not correspond to it, which all great minds have recognized and Kant has presented so admirably. At all events, we can expect to find the answer only in the individual himself and not in the race or its history. This basic problem appears also in all mythology and religion that undertake to explain how evil, sin, guilt came into the world, that is, psychologically speaking, why we must form these ideas. Both mythology and religion answer the question finally by saying that the conscious will, human willing in contrast to natural being, is the root of the arch evil which we designate psychologically as guilt feeling. In the oriental religious systems it is known as evil, in the Jewish as sin, in the Christian as guilt. This transformation is related to the development of conscious willing just outlined whose first externalization we recognized as a denial, a negation. On account of its negative origin the will is always evil as, for example, with Schopenhauer who harks back to the corresponding oriental teachings. The idea of sin as the biblical presentation teaches, is related to the next developmental level where will, consciously defiant, is affirmed, that is, where knowledge thereof already introduces pride. Finally the Christian idea of guilt under whose domination we

29

still live just as under that of the Jewish idea of sin, is the reaction to the positively creative will tendencies of man, to his presumption in wanting to be not only omniscient like God, but to be God himself, a creator.

Here one might be tempted to think of Freud's "father complex" and to derive this creative will from the Œdipus complex. This, however, would be to leave the actually creative unexplained, a lack of psychoanalytic comprehension which Freud himself has seen and admitted. For Freud, that which we call "will" originates, as it were, in the father identification, in the wish to be in the father's place. But this conception itself in my opinion is nothing other than a denial of the own will, which is ascribed to the father (identification) or to God. For Adler again, the will, crudely put, is not father identification, but father protest, the wanting to be otherwise, which again is only a method of interpretation—even if a correct one. Actually the will is both, or rather neither. It is indeed positive and negative, will and counter-will, in the same individual at the same time, as I have already expressed it, principally in "Der Künstler." The will, in a certain stage of development is projected upon the father, is objectified in him, because the father represents a strong will, because he in actuality represents a symbol of the will or resistance to it. The real problem lies in man himself, beyond identification, beyond the biological, and guilt feeling comes not primarily because one wants to put himself in the father's place which one ought not to do, but because in developing, one *must* become father, creator, and will not. The authentic psychological problem, therefore, lies in this, whence the "ought not" on the one side, and the "will not" on the other.

Just as the father is not the prototype of will but only its symbolic representative—and not the first even then—so God too is not simply a deified father as Freud will have it, but an ideal created in man's image, in a word, a projection of the consciously willing ego. This religious justification turns out much more nobly just because the actual father, who is only a weak representative of the will is thereby ignored, and does not disturb the nobility of the ego projection. The father, therefore, is only a first modest personification of conscious will which soon is not satisfied with this real representative but symbolizes its next

30

great developmental step in the creative, all powerful and all knowing God. In the religious myths, the creative will appears personified in God, and man already feels himself guilty when he assumes himself to be like God, that is, ascribes this will to himself. In the heroic myths on the contrary, man appears as himself creative and guilt for his suffering and fall is ascribed to God, that is, to his own will. Both are only extreme reaction phenomena of man wavering between his Godlikeness and his nothingness, whose will is awakened to knowledge of its power and whose consciousness is aroused to terror before it. The heroic myth strives to justify this creative will through glorifying its deeds, while religion reminds man that he himself is but a creature dependent on cosmic forces. So the creative will automatically brings the guilt reaction with it, as the self reducing depression follows the manic elation. In a word, will and guilt are the two complementary sides of one and the same phenomenon, which Schopenhauer, resting on the Hindoo teachings, has perceived and comprehended most deeply of all moderns. A philosophy of will accordingly must either be deeply pessimistic if it emphasizes the guilt side, or extremely optimistic like Nietzsche if it affirms its creative power.

In psychoanalysis we find both aspects but not harmoniously united, rather they stand side by side as one of the numerous unreconciled contradictions. As therapy, analysis is optimistic, believes as it were in the good in men and in some kind of capacity for and possibility of salvation. In theory it is pessimistic; man has no will and no creative power, is driven by the id and repressed by the super-ego authorities, is unfree and still guilty. Here lies before us so transparent a contradiction that one can only wonder how it was possible and must again recognize therein a psychological problem so fundamental that it leads far beyond a critique of psychoanalysis. Free will belongs to the idea of guilt or sin as inevitably as day to night, and even if there were none of the numerous proofs for the inner freedom of the conscious will, the fact of human consciousness of guilt alone would be sufficient to prove the freedom of will as we understand it psychologically beyond a doubt. We say man reacts *as if* he were guilty, but if he reacts so it is because he is guilty psychologically, feels himself responsible, consequently no psychoanalysis in the

world can relieve him of this guilt feeling by any reference to
complexes however archaic. Therefore one should not only permit the individual to will but actually guide him to willing in
order at least to justify constructively the guilt feeling which he
can by no means escape. I do not mean by rationalizations, religious, pedagogic or therapeutic, but through his own creative
action, through the deed itself.

At this point we can formulate whence the guilt feeling arises
and what it means. We have contrasted will and consciousness
previously and have seen that now the one, now the other is interpreted as "bad" or "false," according to whether the experience side or the knowledge side is emphasized, and depending upon
the momentary overweighting of the one sphere by the other. In
the conscious perception of will phenomena the knowledge side
is emphasized; in the immediate content of willing, it is the experience side. Only when the moral evaluation "bad," which restrains the individual in the experience of childhood, is trans-
ferred from the content of willing to the will itself, does the
ethical conflict within the individual arise out of the external
will conflict and this, through the denial of the own will, finally
leads to consciousness of guilt. However, guilt is also determined
on the will side and this double source makes it a strong invincible
power. For against this supremacy of consciousness which sets
up for the individual himself the ethical norms of right and wrong
(not the moral ones of good and bad) the will reacts with a condemnation of consciousness, which it perceives as restriction, and
this is the state of affairs which we describe as consciousness of
guilt. In this sense guilt consciousness is simply a consequence
of conciousness, or more correctly, it is the self-consciousness
of the individual as of one willing consciously. As the Fall presents it—knowing is sin, knowledge creates guilt. Consciousness,
which restrains the will through its ethical norms, is perceived
by the latter to be just as bad as the individual's own will is seen
to be by consciousness. Guilt consciousness is therefore actually
a consequence of increased self-consciousness, yes at bottom is
just this in its most fateful working out as conscience. We cannot occupy ourselves here with the different possibilities and
forms of the restriction of consciousness upon the one side and
the repression of will upon the other, although this makes com-

prehensible the different forms and degrees of the so-called neurotic reactions.[1] It is important here to recognize that the neurotic type represents not a form of illness but the most individualistic beings of our age in whom awareness of the concepts, badness, sin, guilt, has finally developed into tormenting self-consciousness of this relationship.

The neurotic type of our age, whom we meet in places other than the consulting room of the neurologist and the treatment room of the analyst, is therefore only the further development of that negative human type which has existed as long as the will has existed in our mental lives, and shows one side of this conflict in extreme form. It is the man in whom is manifested a will as strong as that of the creative man of action, only in the neurotic patient this will expresses itself in its original negative character, as counter-will, and at the same time is perceived through the medium of conscious knowledge as consciousness of guilt. The so-called neurotics, therefore, do not represent a class of sick people, upon the cure of whom society must concentrate; they represent rather the extreme outgrowth of the modern type of man, whose cure both individually and socially is possible only in one and the same way—no matter whether this ensues in the form of an individual therapy, a general educational reform or finally on the ground of a world view, the basis of which is formed by knowledge of the state of affairs just described. At all events, for individual as for social therapy, a world view is indispensable and the more one strives against this presupposition the less prospect one has of finding a solid basis for educational reforms or therapeutic results. Yes, one is surprised how this comes to pass of itself if one does not set out to want to make the person other than he is, but permits him to be what he is, without his needing to feel guilty or inferior on account of it. The neurotic type, which we all represent to a certain extent, suffers from the fact that he cannot accept himself, cannot endure himself and will have it otherwise. The therapy accordingly cannot be corrective but only affirmative; it must transform him from a negative person of suffering and guilt to a positive man of will and action, which he was in the beginning even if his soul life has be-

[1] See also in this connection the chapter "Likeness and Difference" in Book I of "Will Therapy."

come ever more complicated and painful with the increase of consciousness.

We are, therefore, human beings, who through consciousness, through too much self-knowledge are restricted or hindered in living, a type which Shakespeare pictured psychologically in such a masterly fashion in Hamlet, who in our age for the first time has found complete recognition. We must not forget, however, that knowledge also has a creative side, as for example, Shakespeare himself shows in the creation of the Hamlet figure. Evidently he himself represented the Hamlet type, which did not hinder him, unlike his hero, from using his conflict creatively instead of perceiving it merely as a restriction. Knowing, therefore, when it works creatively, can be a substitute for living, yes itself a form of experiencing. It becomes then an inner victory of will if one may speak thus, instead of an outer, but it is a victory of will which the individual must pay for in every case with some kind of deficit. The active hero who represents the conscious power of will can act because he knows only his will, not its origin and motives; he comes to grief just in this, that he cannot foresee the consequences of his act. The passive man of suffering cannot act because his self-consciousness restricts his will which manifests itself as guilt feeling in the face of the deed. The spiritually creative type which I have characterized as "artist," lives in constant conflict between these two extreme possibilities. The artist solves it for himself and others since he transposes the will affirmation creatively into knowledge, that is, expresses his will spiritually and changes the unavoidable guilt feeling into ethical ideal formation, which spurs him on and qualifies him for ever higher performance in terms of self-development.

IV

TRUTH AND REALITY

*"Nur der Irrtum ist das Leben,
Und das Wissen ist der Tod."*

"Only in Error is there Life;
Knowledge is Death." — SCHILLER

IN THE previous chapters we have elaborated the contrast between knowing and experiencing in terms of the development of consciousness from a tool of will and an instrument of will affirmation, to the tormenting self-consciousness of the modern individual. Knowledge in the sense of self knowledge leads finally to constant awareness of itself, and since it is always present in immediate experience too, disturbs it grievously if it does not block it completely. To this development of consciousness into the neurotic self restriction of living there corresponds the general evolution of the neurosis from a basic will problem to a problem of consciousness.[1] If in the first place, the will was bad and its denial to blame for all suffering, now conscious knowledge about ourselves and our problems, in other words the insight into this denial process, constitutes the evil, the sin, or the guilt.

The problem of consciousness has yet another aspect which is opposed to this termination in tormenting self-consciousness and this is consciousness as a source of pleasure. Consciousness originally as a tool of the will and an instrument for its accomplishment or for justification is a source of pleasure just as is the carrying out of will itself. Yes, the consciousness which confirms will and approves of its accomplishment is the very source of pleasure. In this psychological sense, pleasure and displeasure are actually only two opposite conscious aspects of will phenomena. The putting over of will in living plus the consciousness of it in experience is the mechanism of the pleasure feeling which

[1] See in this connection "Will Therapy," Book I, chap. v.

35

we call happiness. It is at once a double, really a redoubled enjoyment, first in the act of will itself and again in the reflecting mirror of consciousness which says "yes" once more to the will achievement. Only when consciousness is placed in the service of the counter-will and manifests itself as a tendency to repression or denial, do we feel unpleasantness and experience in the summation of painful feeling and the simultaneous consciousness thereof, the sense of pain contrasted with pleasure which also rep · resents a reflection phenomenon of consciousness. Both reactions relate to the present attitude of consciousness, to the will expression revealed in experience. Knowledge, on the contrary, is more an historical process, which follows experience and feeling, although it is often very immediate. Knowledge separates consciousness from experiencing, or rather is itself a consequence of this separation and has the tendency to preserve the pleasurable, to remember it and to deny and forget the painful.

Why this never quite succeeds is not only the problem of the neurosis, but of all human suffering. In other words. how does it happen that consciousness turns from an organ for pleasure in the service of will fulfilment into an organ of pain in consequence of will denial. I believe this comes about because consciousness from the beginning has a negative character, just as will originally is negative, denying. The negative side of consciousness, however, is its connection with reality, just as the will also emerges as counter-will on the reality of the strange will. Consciousness originally by means of the sense organs is the mediator of reality, of the real world, and as such has the capacity to cause pain, like reality. It opposes the will accordingly as reality does (for example in morals) because originally and even further it is the psychic representative, not only of will, but also of reality. In other words, consciousness is intensified reality which we perceive with pain as long as and insofar as the will is not able to put it into its service, to overcome it, which it strives to do with outside reality also. In this sense all is real that opposes itself to our will as invincible resistance, whether it be outer reality or the inner reality of consciousness.

In order to come from this reality side to the inner truth side of consciousness, we must take a further step in the building up of the will psychology and approach the difficult sphere of the

emotional life. For the area in which all these will and consciousness phenomena take place perceived in sense terms as pleasure
and pain, or spiritually as happiness and sorrow, is the emotional sphere standing equally close to will and consciousness
where all these activities come together and flow into one another.
The emotional life represents accordingly the strongest inner
force. It is even stronger than the sexual instinct which is always
capable of being controlled and satisfied somehow. Not so the
emotional life, which is uncontrollable and insatiable, yes, whose
very essence consists of its inability to be controlled or satisfied.

If we consider first the relation of the emotional life to the
sphere of will, we find that it is a two-fold one. All that we designate as emotion in the narrower sense of the word, love, gratitude,
longing, tenderness, is finally only the breaking, or rather the
softening of the will. It is not that we subject our own will to the
will of the other by means of emotion, but rather our own softened
will is the emotion itself, a kind of self subjection, in the face of
our pride. The defense against this yielding of self-will we perceive as shame, the affirmation of it as love, and the denial as hate,
a kind of hardening of the will. Here we touch upon the second
side of the relation of will to the emotional life, namely, the
affects. For what I call affect is a kind of warding off of emotion, actually an attempt to guide it back into the sphere of will
as psychic action, while emotion is passive. Scorn, anger, hate
are affirmations, exaggerations of the negative will which sets
itself against the rising softening influence of emotion by divert-
ing it into the sphere of will as a defense. On the other hand, the
affirmation of emotion through the will, or better said, its release
into emotion, leads not to subjection to the other, but to that
which we call surrender, a kind of beneficent release of will.

We must postpone a discussion of the relation of the emotional
life to the sexual life which is so often emphasized but has never
been understood, to the chapter on "Happiness and Redemption"
in order to turn now to the relation of the emotional sphere to
consciousness. Of the affirmation of will-hardening manifested
in the affect, there is only this to be said, that it momentarily
overpowers consciousness in order afterwards to force it to
justify the affect expression. Where this does not succeed, the
originally denied emotion appears afterwards in the reaction of

repentance, which often leads to the complete breaking of will. The influence of emotion as a will phenomenon upon the sphere of consciousness shows itself where will denies the emotional yielding, without increasing it to full denial in an affect. This partial denial is certainly not without influence upon the emotional sphere itself, where it manifests itself as the transformation of positive emotion (love) into guilt feeling, thus again proving guilt to be the result of miscarried denial. The influence upon consciousness is a manifold, to a large extent a grave one, which affects not only all of our behavior but also our thinking and so leads us back to the theme "Truth and Reality."

The original nature of denial is seen in the attempt to oppose to a painful reality, the power of the individual will. Soon, however, the denial mechanism is turned entirely inward where it expresses itself in the emotional sphere as affect and in the sphere of consciousness as repression. This leads secondarily then to all the thought processes which we know as distortion, rationalization, justification and doubt. Repression as I have already shown before [1] is denial continued in conscious thought and appears when the individual becomes aware of emotional denial and wants to repress the associated memory content in order to be free of the feeling (which however has its origin in the sphere of will not consciousness). This repression can fail of its purpose or succeed only partially and then doubt sets in, which brings into question the reality of what has been thought, that is, the truth, since it can neither repress it consciously, nor deny it emotionally. Doubt, therefore, is originally intended to shake truth, it is the intellectual struggle for truth, for certainty. This, however, is nothing other than the old battle lifted from the sphere of will and emotion into the sphere of consciousness and is conducted with the same inevitability and stubbornness as the original will conflict itself. Accordingly no argument avails against doubt because truth is what it avoids, just as no arguments convince the counter-will, of which doubt is only the intellectual manifestation.

If doubt represents the conscious counter-will, truth represents the will intellectually. Crudely put, one might say: "What I will

[1] See the chapter "Verleugnung und Realitätsanpassung" in "Genetische Psychologie" Part I.

is true, that is, what I make truth," or to be banal, "what I want to believe." Also here again the problem is not one of content, namely to decide what *the* truth is, but rather what truth is and this setting of the problem contains the solution in itself just as the laconic answer of Pilate to the announcement of Jesus that he had come to bring the truth. Truth, however, is not only a subjective concept and accordingly a psychological problem, but it is an emotion like its opposite doubt, which has long been recognized as such. Both have nothing to do with reality except that both stand in opposition to it. Truth is what I believe or affirm, doubt is denial, or rejection. But the reality which penetrates consciousness through our sense organs can influence us only by way of the emotional life and becomes either truth or falsehood accordingly; that is, is stamped as psychic reality or unreality. In the interaction of will and consciousness as it manifests itself in the emotional life we find a continuous influencing of one sphere by the other. Even the purely sensory consciousness is not merely receptive, but is guided and restricted by will. I see or hear what I want to, not what is. What is can only be learned by overcoming the tendency to deny all that I do not want to see or hear or perceive. Still more clearly is intellect influenced by will, for logical, causally directed thinking, going beyond the effort to shut out the painful is the positive, active expression of the will to control reality. The third level of creative consciousness or phantasy, is the most positive expression of the counter-will, which not only says "I will *not* perceive what is," but "I will that it is otherwise, i.e. just as I want it. And this, only this is truth."

Truth therefore is the conscious concomitant, yes, the affirmation of the constructive or creative completion of will on the intellectual level, just as we understand the perception of pleasure as the emotional affirmation of will expression. Accordingly truth brings intellectual pleasure as doubt brings intellectual pain. Truth as positive emotional experience means "it is good, that I will is right, is pleasurable." It is, therefore, willing itself the affirmation of which creates intellectual pleasure. That we do not know truth in its psychological nature but set it up as it were outside of every psychology, yes, as the criterion of psychology itself, as again related to its content. If we did not do that, this last intellectual way to justify will, the will to truth as a drive to knowledge which shall make an end of doubt would also be denied us. Once more we cannot enjoy completely the pleasure of truth seeking because it is an expression of our own will which even here on the level of knowledge and self knowledge needs the content of a general truth equally valid for all, in order to deny its own truth, its own individuality. And here, in my opinion, we hit upon the most paradoxical phenomenon of the human soul, the understanding of which I consider the most important result of my relativity theory of knowledge. It concerns the law of continuous development of our general psychological knowledge. This results not as one might think pedagogically, by the handing over and broadening of the already known, whereby he who follows knows more or sees better. No, it is not only that he knows more, he knows differently because he himself is different. And this "being different" is related to the continuous development of self consciousness, which alters the whole individuality because it determines it. This knowing differently about ourselves, about our own psychic processes is in this sense only a new interpretation of ourselves, with which and in which we free ourselves from the old, the bygone, the past, and above all from our own past. Creative individuals, in their advancing knowledge, represent therefore only the increased self knowledge of mounting self consciousness which manifests itself in them. Only in this sense can *their* truth also serve as *the* truth and not in relation to any extra-psychological content of the truth-emotion which transforms the positive affirmation of willing into conviction.

With this separation of the content of truth from the feeling of trueness, there is revealed to us the problem of truth and reality in its complete practical meaning, as well as in its psychological and epistemological aspect. The only "trueness" in terms of actual psychic reality is found in emotion, not in thinking, which at best denies or rationalizes truth, and not necessarily in action unless it follows from feeling and is in harmony with it. This, however, is seldom the case because the will for the most part does not permit it but preserves for itself the supremacy over the sphere of action. Then, however, action ensues either on the basis of conscious thought guided by will or is the expression of an affect and is, therefore, not emotionally true in either case. For the most part it stands thus, that the denial tendency arising from the negative origin of will and ruling our entire spiritual life in the sphere of thought and action, particularly as far as it concerns our relations to other people, manifests itself as self-deception concerning its own emotions, but really is the truth. The paradox therein is this, that exactly what we pretend consciously to be the truth, this it actually is psychically. It is only that we attach to emotion, as it were, this intellectual denial in order not to admit it to ourselves and the other. Again the will—in its negative form—presses in past emotion and must deny even while it sanctions it. This is the psychological side of the situation. In relation to practical action, to behavior, the result is that we pride ourselves on playing a role when it has to do with true emotional reaction. We actually play, then, what we are in truth, but perceive it as untrue, as false, because again we cannot accept ourselves without rationalization. Just so, in the exaggeration of an action or reaction, the more genuine it is, the more we perceive it as voluntary exaggeration. (I play the injured role, means, I am injured.)

The understanding of this relation between truth and reality is not only highly important psychologically as it reveals to us the psychic truth-status of lying, pretension, dramatization, but also practically for judging the actions resulting therefrom. This explains why we rightly judge a man by his actions and these again according to their manifest appearance, as not only the laity but also justice and education do. For the psychic motivation, upon which one finally stumbles with careful analysis, may be psychically true but it is not actually like the act itself whose psychological understanding always includes its interpretation in terms of the will-guilt problem. Accordingly, therefore, the so-called Freudian slip is psychologically truer than the correct behavior which always rests on a denial of what we really want to do and which usually comes through only in blunders where at the same time it is made ineffective, as also in the dream through the sleeper's incapacity for action. Here also light falls upon the peculiar phenomenon of the intentional blunder, in whose mechanism the emotionally true intention again betrays itself. In this sense the majority of our actions as we have previously described in conscious acting, pretending, falsehood, are really would-be slips.

From this results not only a new comprehension of human behavior, but also an understanding of it, a view of life that is therapeutic in an anti-analytic sense. It is to the effect that our seeking the truth in human motives for acting and thinking is destructive. With the truth, one cannot live. To be able to live one needs illusions, not only outer illusions such as art, religion, philosophy, science and love afford, but inner illusions which first condition the outer. The more a man can take reality as truth, appearance as essence, the sounder, the better adjusted, the happier will he be. At the moment when we begin to search after truth we destroy reality and our relation to it. Be it that we find in the beloved person in truth a substitute for the mother, or for another person, or for ourselves. Be it that, just reversed, we establish through analysis that we really love the hated person, but must displace this love upon another person, because our proud will does not permit that we confess this to ourselves. In a word, the displacements are the real. Reality unveils itself to analysis always as something displaced, psychologically untrue. This is a cognitive fact but no life principle. It is not at all a matter of putting an end to these displacements because it is impossible as the analytic situation teaches us best of all, where the patient only continues this displacement process further, in denying the actual feeling relation to the analyst, and displacing it upon other persons or situations. This displacement, if it succeeds, we regard and rightly so as healing, for this constantly effective process of self-deceiving, pretending and blundering, is no psychopathological mechanism, but the essence of reality, the—as it were—continuous blunder. This is also the authentic wisdom of the Greek Œdipus myth, whose hero would live happily in his displaced world of appearance if he were not driven by his intellectual pride, the will to truth, to expose his reality as lies, as appearance, as falsehood. He carries out his will pleasurably in the search for truth, in the overcoming of obstacles, but suffers in the content of what he finds, which brings to consciousness the denied emotions (in the case of Œdipus, for his parents).

From this conception there results a paradoxical but deep insight into the essence of the neurosis. If man is the more normal, healthy and happy, the more he can accept the appearance of reality as truth, that is, the more successfully he can repress, displace, deny, rationalize, dramatize himself and deceive others, then it follows that the suffering of the neurotic comes not from a painful reality but from painful truth which only secondarily makes reality unbearable. Spiritually the neurotic has been long since where psychoanalysis wants to bring him without being able to, namely at the point of seeing through the deception of the world of sense, the falsity of reality. He suffers, not from all the pathological mechanisms which are psychically necessary for living and wholesome but in the refusal of these mechanisms which is just what robs him of the illusions important for living. The neurotic, as distinguished from the creative man of will whom the hero Œdipus represents on the intellectual level, is not the voluntary happy seeker of truth, but the forced, unhappy finder of it. He seeks, moreover, no general objective truth, and finds his own subjective truth, which runs like this—"I am so little and bad and weak and worthless that I cannot deceive myself about myself, cannot accept myself as a worthwhile individual."

While the average well adjusted man can make the reality that is generally accepted as truth into his own truth, the creative searcher after truth seeks and finds his own truth which he then wants to make general—that is, real. He creates his reality, as it were, from his truth. The neurotic, on the other hand, finds his subjective truth but cannot accept it as such and destroys therewith the given reality, that is, the pleasurable relation to it, as he is neither in position to make it his truth nor to translate his truth into reality. The difference lies again in the attitude or rather in the kind of consciousness, in its relation to will. The average man has reality consciousness more strongly developed, the creative type will consciousness, the neurotic individual self-consciousness. Reality consciousness comes from adaptation of will, the creative phantasy consciousness from will affirmation, the neurotic self consciousness from will denial. The will itself is justified in the first case, generally and socially; in the second case, individually and ethically; in the third case it is denied.

The differing quality of conscious attitude to the will problem which decides the predominance of pleasure or pain, of destruction or construction, depends essentially upon the funda-

mental significance of the content problem. Reality consciousness is predominantly oriented from the standpoint of content;
its truth is, as already said, the actual, and is therefore ex-
clusively content. The creative consciousness is also contentual
but in distinction employs predominantly subjective material,
phantasies of every kind, which in the last analysis represent
will phenomena. The neurotic self consciousness, on the contrary,
busies itself in an introspective way, which we can only designate
as psychological, with the psychic processes themselves, and they
consequently represent his predominant content. Certainly the
neurotic also has real content and phantasy content, of the first
too little, of the latter too much, but the essential thing in his
form of consciousness is still the introspective self-consciousness
of the psychic processes as such. Also in this sense and on this account, the neurotic is much nearer to actual truth psychologically than the others and it is just that from which he suffers.

Psychoanalytic therapy then works therapeutically for the
neurotic in that it offers him new contents for the justification
of his will in the form of scientific "truth." It works therefore on
the basis of illusion exactly like religion, art, philosophy and
love, the great spontaneous psychotherapies of man, as I called
them in "Der Künstler." On the other hand, the psychotherapy
which lets the individual first of all accept himself and through
that learn to accept reality, must also, according to its nature,
use illusions not truth in the psychological sense because it is
that from which the neurotic suffers. In this sense, psychoanalysis too is therapeutic but only so long or with those individuals
who are still capable of this degree of illusion and with a class
of neurotics whom we see today, this is often no longer possible.
The insoluble conflict in which psychoanalysis itself is caught
arises because it wants to be theory and therapy at the same time
and this is just as irreconcilable as truth with reality. As psychological theory it seeks truth, that is, insight into psychic
processes themselves and this works destructively, as neurotic
self consciousness shows only too clearly. As therapy it must
offer the patient contentual consolations and justifications which
again cannot be psychologically true, or, as far as they are
true, cannot work therapeutically.

This brings us back again to the part played by the will problem in the neurosis. This disintegrating destructive character of self consciousness arises in the last analysis from the original negative character of will which works itself out, not only toward the outside as resistance, but also toward the inside as counter-will. The destructive element enters first through denial, negation, and finally relates to our emotions, that is, to ourselves. Here the psychology of the neuroses branches off and can be comprehended only as the opposite of the psychology of the creative individual who confirms his will and himself but not in terms of the psychology of the average man. The fundamental methodological error of Freudian psychology is that it is oriented therapeutically on the psychology of the normal man and knows the creative only in its negative expression as neurosis. The Freudian psychology pictures the man as he would be if he were normal, healthy, but the mistake lies in this that the neurotic individual cannot be made normal and healthy in this way, but only through the positive, creative affirmation of will, which the moralistic pedagogical therapist wants to translate into normal adaptation. The neurotic loses out, however, because of the relation to reality, because he knows too much truth about himself, no matter whether this manifests itself as guilt consciousness, inferiority feeling, or incapacity for love. It is at bottom always only incapacity for illusion, but an incapacity for illusion which concerns the sphere of will in the same way as it does the sphere of consciousness both of which the creative type affirms, while the normal man does not perceive them at all as separated forces which oppose one another. The neurotic not only turns his consciousness as a self-tormenting introspection toward the inside but he also turns his will as counter-will inside instead of putting it outside like the constructive man of action. With him it is not only denial of painful reality or rather of painful emotion which makes reality resistant to him, but it is the denial of feeling in general through the will which finally excuses the denying factor itself, i.e. the counter-will, on moral grounds, or rationalizes it ethically and accordingly either suffers from guilt feeling or from the breaking of the will, or both. He must then explain, motivate, understand, rationalize, justify each of his acts of will, whether positive or negative, instead of simply affirming them, which makes homo sapiens into that thought specialist among living beings, whose extreme developmental type we have before us in the classic form of the neurosis of our time, the compulsion neurosis.

On the other side, this tendency to deny will expressions and the need to justify the denial has led to all the creations of genius, as we know them from the religious formation of heroes to philosophic ethics. These universal justification therapies fail before the all destroying self consciousness which is no longer capable of illusions and unsparingly exposes even the last great attempt of this kind, psychoanalysis, as it has all earlier ones because it seeks to give at one and the same time comforting contents which no longer delude and psychological truth which does not comfort. Therefore not only must every effective therapy be purely subjective, because of the difference of individualities and the corresponding neurotic types, it must also be relative because we all represent this neurotic type of intensified self consciousness whose destruction of reality, of truth, of illusion and of itself, we are only now experiencing in its full strength. We find ourselves in a transition period in which we still seek mightily for new illusions without being able to utilize them therapeutically just as we struggle violently for truth about ourselves which makes us ever more unhappy. Psychoanalysis, as I have said, gives both. This was its strength and becomes more and more its weakness, the more it is dragged into this irresistible knowledge process of hyperconsciousness.

This process has now reached a point in the sphere of consciousness which the neurotic type shows equally clearly. Parallel with the denial of feeling, as we have just described it, there goes also the denial of consciousness and indeed to the degree that the awareness of inner truth approaches something we do not want to see because it is painful and destructive. The stronger denial tendency of the neurotic therefore is also a defense mechanism against this domination by self consciousness which must know the truth without the individual's wanting it. The neurotic type of our day, therefore, must rather learn not to see the inner truth about himself, not to have to see it, as his self consciousness represents only a manifestation of the negative will. When he can again will positively and translate this into action or creative achievement, then his self consciousness does not need to torment itself with the question why it cannot will or to create his thinking in justification of this will. Here also a positive basis of his will to truth becomes apparent. Truth is to free from doubt, from the insecurity of our whole system of thought which is built up on interpretative negativism, as represented in the endless rationalizations of our will and consciousness motives. Here again truth as inner emotional experience opposes the uncertainty of reality and the thought processes corresponding to it. In the inner awareness of our true feelings the neurotic self consciousness manifests itself in its most tormenting form, in the objectified content of truth we have found the last greatest comfort of illusion, of which the self conscious type of our age is still capable. Its positive affirmation corresponds to a pleasurable act of will; its subjective perception which is related to the emotional life, is painful, sorrowful; its constructive transformation into a general truth, although actually representing an illusion, is creative.

V

SELF AND IDEAL

"This above all: to thine own self be true."
—SHAKESPEARE

WE RETURN now to the presentation of the inner will conflict, particularly as it is manifested in its effect on the ethical ideal formation. In the analytic situation we see and feel the will of the patient as "resistance" to our will, just as the child breaks his will on the will of the parents and at the same time strengthens it. But the analysis of the adult gives us this advantage, that we can throw this resistance back upon the individual himself, provided we work constructively; that is, we can show the patient that he actually suffers from a purely inner conflict between will and consciousness, but analysis enables him to project it as an outward one. Now the form and manner in which this inner conflict appears and what effects it produces within and without, constitute the actual subject matter of the will psychology, which is to be independent of moral, pedagogic and social viewpoints. The latter we must examine in their turn in judging those situations where we are concerned with the collision of one will with another or with the will of the group. Just now we have to do rather with individual consciousness and particularly with that aspect of it which expresses itself positively and constructively as ideal formation.

As we are interested here only in the positive, constructive, creative side of the conflict, and indeed only with a specific form of it, it is necessary to remind ourselves that we must ascribe even to the positive will a negative origin with whose genesis we have busied ourselves elsewhere. Long since, especially in the first part of "Genetische Psychologie," I have pointed out the significance of the mechanism of denial for all thinking and acting. In this denial there is evidenced as I would like to emphasize now, the original negative nature of will power, which, as Goethe puts it "always intends the bad and constantly creates the good." At all events we see man in various situations, but especially in the so-called neurotic reactions, think and act as if he were ruled by two wills which struggle against each other, as formerly the own will struggled against an external, opposing will. These two factors which lie at the root of all dualistic world views, from the Persian Zarathustrianism to the system of Schopenhauer, were described by Freud in the beginning as the conscious and the unconscious, later with a deepened meaning, as the ego and the id. Accordingly unconsciousness was at first identified with sexuality, consciousness with the ego; while Freud later desexualized the id somewhat or rather made it more cosmic, on the other hand he ascribed to the ego unconscious elements also. This connecting of new terminology with old contents is more confusing than clarifying, especially as the ego plays a relatively slight role with Freud despite its unconscious elements because it is ruled by the two great powers, the id and the super-ego, which represents the moral code. I have no occasion to go back to this terminology here, because I would like to describe the phenomena just as they present themselves to me, except to make clear where and in how far my conception differs from the former one.

I see and understand the two opposing powers in the individual as the same forces that are experienced as a conflict of wills in the clash of two individuals, namely, will forces. The one force is that which we experience in impact with the outside world, namely, our conscious will. But what is the other inner force against which it strives, or rather, which strives against it, for this seems to me to be the real situation. One might say that this is sexuality, as Freud originally assumed, provided one understands it not only in a broader but in the broadest sense of the word. Accordingly we say in biological terms the generic in contrast to the individual in which case the question remains open as to whether or not one should include the collective racial which in Jung's meaning is a social-ethical concept. At all events we need no external sexual prohibition, no castration trauma, as our daily experience with children shows, to explain the struggle of the individual ego, the conscious will, against sexuality, against generic compulsion. The parents or others in authority may represent to the child powerful wills but one can oppose them openly or secretly, one can finally overcome them, perhaps can even free oneself from them or escape them. Sexuality, however, as it awakens in the individual about the time of puberty is an incomparably stronger power than all the external authorities put together. Were it not so, the world would have died out long since.

This generic sexual compulsion which, as sexual attraction, is the root of the Freudian Œdipus complex, when it is actually completely aroused, naturally goes beyond parental boundaries because generally it goes beyond all bounds. It is so strong and dominates the individual so extremely that soon he begins to defend himself against its domination, just because it is a domination, something that interferes dictatorially with his own will as individual, appearing as a new, alien and more powerful counter-will just as the ego is strengthened by puberty. The reason the individual defends himself so strongly against it is because the biological sex drive would force him again under the rule of a strange will, of the sexual will of the "other," while the ego has only just begun at this time to breathe a little freely out from under the pressure of strange authoritative wills. Accordingly he flees of necessity to a mechanism for the satisfaction of urgent sexuality that enables him to maintain the newly won autonomy at least a little while without subjecting himself to an alien sexual will. I speak of the typical masturbation conflict of this and also of later years which represents nothing but the powerful expression of the conflict between the individual will and generic will manifesting itself here as sex drive. This struggle always ends with the victory of the individual. Although he must often pay too dearly for it, nevertheless an ego victory it is, since the very appearance of masturbation registers a successful attempt to put the sexual instinct under the control of the individual will.

These individuals even when they present themselves as weak willed, falling into vice without resistance, are at bottom people of unusually strong wills who have merely concentrated their wills for the moment in the one direction. They often succeed in becoming master of the sexual urge to such an extent that they can suppress it through conscious effort of will, and can

also arouse and satisfy it; that is, when the individual wills it
and not when sexuality wills it. Only, as Adler believes, they must
continue to prove this will power of theirs and that gives the
appearance of not being able to get free of the sex drive. This
appearance is correct too, insofar as it is based on a denial of
will power which we could here bring into the universal formula:
I do not want to will at all, but I must. In contrast to Adler,
however, I do not believe that the individual must continuously
prove his own strength of will because he feels inferior, and
therefore is really weak. I believe much more that he could never
prove his strength if he were not actually strong, if he did not
have just that powerful a will. Here again the problem is why
the individual cannot accept his own will, cannot admit it or
affirm it, but is compelled to reject and deny it, in other words,
to replace it with a "must." But just this denial tendency brings
with it secondarily the guilt and inferiority feeling which really
says, "I ought not to have such a strong will, or in general any
will at all." In this sense, the powerful compulsion of the biological sexual urge is raised to a representative of the will, whose
individual freedom is then justified by the generic compulsion.
Herein lies the psychological motive for the tie-up of the conscious individual will with the generic sex drive, as significant as
it is fateful, also the origin of the sexual guilt feeling since the
guilt for willing falls into the sexual sphere by displacement and
at the same time is denied and justified.

The explanations that psychoanalysis and also the Adlerian
doctrine give for these phenomena of guilt and inferiority seem
to me unsatisfactory because they do not meet the real problem
at all, that is, the denial of will from which secondarily follow
guilt and inferiority. The explanation given formerly is that
the will of the child has been so broken by the authority of
parents, that it can no longer trust itself to will, in a word, experiences anxiety which was added to it from the outside. Not
only does every educational experiment contradict this, but also
experiences in the psychology of the neuroses and creative per-
sonalities testify that the fact is other and deeper. Our conflicts
in general go back to much deeper causes than external social
restrictions even if we conceive them psychologically with Freud
as internal super-ego formation or with Adler as inner inferi-

ority feeling, springing from the externally inferior status of the child. Probably in the beginning we were bound to our milieu, which, however, we are able to outgrow, and just so to a great extent we have remained bound by nature in our sexual life. But what characterizes man or is made to by himself, perhaps unfortunately, is just the fact that his conscious will increases to a power equal to the outer environmental influences and the inner instinctual claims, and this we must take into account in order to understand the individual in all his reactions. Our will is not only able to suppress the sex urge, but is just as able to arouse it through conscious effort, to increase it and to satisfy it. Perhaps our will is able to do this because it, itself, is a descendant, a representative of the biological will-to-live become conscious, creating itself in self maintenance and reproduction, which in the last analysis is nothing more than supra-individual self maintenance.[1] When this tendency to perpetual self maintenance of the species carries over to the individual, there results the powerful will whose manifestations bring with them guilt reactions because they strive for an enrichment of the individual, biologically at the cost of the species, ethically at the expense of the fellow man.

This brings us to the fundamental thought of my whole viewpoint which I have already expressed in principle in "Der Künstler," namely, that instinct and inhibition, will and counter-will do not correspond to any original dualism, but in the last analysis always represent a kind of inner self limitation of one's own power and, therefore, since everything has its roots within, the outer reflects more than it creates the inner. This conception as was emphasized likewise in "Der Künstler," relates in particular to all kinds of sexual conflicts which arise not through any kind of outer prohibition but through inner inhibition of the own will by the counter-will. It explains also the resistance which Freud's sexual theory has met and necessarily must meet since it is an expression of the same conflict, the understanding of which leads us out of all the futile discussions which psychoanalysis has occasioned. Freud said: "Sexuality is the strong-

[1] See on this point and the following, the beginning of the first chapter in "Der Künstler"—as well as the material on the development of the individual in the introductory chapter of "Genetische Psychologie," Part II, Page 14.

est"; the answer was—"No, the will can control it to a great degree." And both sides were right. But each emphasized only one side, instead of recognizing the relationship between them and understanding the conflict in its essential meaning. Freud has gradually yielded and in his castration and super-ego theory recognizes the power of the factors which inhibit sexuality. But they are for him external anxiety factors and remain so even later, when he internalizes them in the super-ego, although they establish themselves as the court of morals which evokes the uncontrollable guilt reactions. But guilt feeling is something other than internalized anxiety, as it is more than fear of itself, of the claim of instinct, just as the ethical judgments are something more than introjected parental authority.

In order to understand what they are and how they arise, we turn back to the struggle of ego will against race will represented in sexuality, which actually represents a struggle of the child against any pressure that continues within him. In the so-called latency period as Freud has it (between early childhood and puberty) the ego of the individual, his own will, is strengthened and has turned, for the most part in revolutionary reactions, against the parents and other authorities that it has not chosen itself. In the struggle against sexuality which breaks in at that point, the ego, as it were, calls to its aid the earlier contested parental inhibitions and takes them as allies against the more powerful sex drive. This introduction of the will motive makes the mysterious process of the introjection of parental authority comprehensible psychologically for the first time. Hitherto it had to be forced upon the child from the outside and this force must obviously be maintained because the child opposes the acceptance with his will, his counter-will. Moreover the child has no occasion to make of these actual outer restrictions an inner censor, and even if it had reasons, its counter-will would resist the acceptance of force. The child obeys because it wins love, avoids punishment and lessens its own inner control. But it does not do these things of its own free will; on the contrary, prohibition strengthens the impulse, as we know, just as permission lessens the desire. In puberty, however, where the individual is awakened on the one side to autonomy of will and on the other defends himself against the pressure of the racial sex urge, he has a strong will motive for making his own these early parental prohibitions and all that he has learned to know meantime in moralistic inhibitions, in order to use them in his encounter with sexuality. Here the individual forms his own super-ego because he needs these moral norms for his own will victory over the sex impulse. Again it is a victory which many a time is bought at too dear a price and must be paid for by a life long dependency on this moral code.

The constructive formation and creative development from what Freud calls super-ego to what I call ideal-formation from the self is a highly complex process which is accomplished in the typical forms of the will conflict and under its pressure. It consists first in the fact that the individual who earlier made his own only externally, limitations accepted of necessity, now affirms them in the service of his own will interests. This affirmation of a condition already established earlier under pressure, is a very important factor psychologically, yes, is *the* essential psychological factor; for the fate of the individual depends on the attitude he takes to the *given* factors, whether these happen to be a part of environment, or the sexual constitution itself. This "I will, because I must," is, as is easily seen, the positive opposite of the denying attitude which we formulated in the sentence, "I do not will at all, but I obey a force!" The whole difference lies in the fact that this force as external cannot be borne and causes the will to react negatively as denial. But if this outer force becomes inner, then there arise two possibilities, the one of which leads to neurotic reactions, the other to ethical standards. If the force although inner is still perceived as force, the will conflict manifests itself, as already pointed out, in guilt feeling, which, as it were, represents an inner ethical compulsion resisting the individual's will just like an alien counter-will. But if the own will says "Yes" to this force, this internal "must," then the inner force becomes inner freedom in that will and counter-will both affirm the same willing.

The process just described goes beyond the mere affirmation of force, either outer or inner, to its constructive evaluation, that is, positively as ethics in ideal-formation and not merely normatively and regulatively. Therefore the individual only takes over the overcome moral code for a protection, as it were, under the first violence of the sexual impulse. Soon, however, the proud will stirs again and strives to win the battle alone without the help of authoritative morality. Here then begins the ethical ideal-formation in the self although the individual may turn to external models, ideal figures from life or history. But these ideals he chooses in terms of his own individuality which, as we know, has nothing to do with infantile authorities, least of all the parents.[1] It does not matter whether the individual succeeds wholly in freeing himself from the traditional moral concepts; probably he never does, especially not as long as he must live with other individuals who more or less depend on this traditional morality. It is important, however, that for everything creative, regardless of how it manifests itself, even in the neurosis, we can thank this striving of the individual, of his individual will to free himself from the traditional moral code and to build his own ethical ideals from himself, ideals which are not only normative for his own personality, but also include the assurance of creative activity of any kind and the possibility of happiness. For this whole process of inner ideal formation which begins with the setting up of one's own moral norms inside is a mighty and important attempt to transform compulsion into freedom. The broader fate of the individual depends essentially on the success with which this attempt is undertaken, how it is carried through and conducted further, also how far it goes in a particular case and where and how it ends.

Certainly it is no planned and straightforward way, but a continuous struggle against outer forces and a constant conflict with inner ones, in which the individual must live through for himself all stages of his evolution. That cannot be avoided and should not be, for just this living through and fighting through constitute the valuable, the constructive, the creative which does not inhibit the will but strengthens and develops it. The first step in the freeing process is that the individual now wills what he was earlier compelled to, what externally or internally he was forced to do, and the normal, average man perhaps never gets beyond this level which guarantees a relatively harmonious working together of will and counter-will. It corresponds to a willed

[1] Certainly not with the parents of the hero, the man of strong will, as I explained in the "Myth of the Birth of the Hero."

acceptance of the external compulsion of authority, the moral code and the inner compulsion of the sexual instinct. Accordingly it permits fewer possibilities of conflict but also fewer creative possibilities of any kind. The human being to a large extent is one with himself and with the surrounding world and feels himself to be a part of it. He has the consciousness of individuality but at the same time also the feeling of likeness, of unity, which makes the relation to the outer world pleasant.

The next stage is characterized by the feeling of division in the personality, through the disunity of will and counter-will, which means a struggle (moral) against the compulsion of the outer world as well as an inner conflict between the two wills. The constructive person goes beyond the mere moralistic and instinctual affirmation of the obligatory in his own ideal formation which itself having become a new goal-seeking power can work thereafter constructively or inhibitingly. On this level there are possibilities of neurotic or creative development not present on the first level. And again it depends on what position the will takes toward the moral and ethical standards originally called in by it or self created, after they have once been called into life, or have even achieved power. So the will is always compelled to take attitudes anew; first to the given, then to the self created, and finally even to the willed. And this taking an attitude can always turn out to be negative or positive, negative even when it concerns something originally self willed or self created. This negative attitude in turn can always have one of two results; either it leads to improvement, to a higher level, to a new creativity as with the productive, or it creates itself in self criticism, guilt and inferiority feeling, in short, under the neurotic inhibition of will.

The third and highest level of development is characterized by a unified working together of the three fully developed powers, the will, the counter-will and the ideal formation born from the conflict between them which itself has become a goal-setting, goal-seeking, force. Here the human being, the genius, is again at one with himself; what he does, he does fully and completely in harmony with all his powers and his ideals. He knows no hesitation, and no doubt as does the conflicted man of the second level, even though the latter be productive. He is a man of will and deed in accord with himself, although as distinguished from the type of realistic man he is not in accord with the world, because too different from others. I do not mean that the conflicts of this type would be more of an external nature, played out more in the battle with the hostile environment; I merely wish to emphasize here the creative side of their being, which just through its unlikeness to reality gives to genius its peculiar greatness. This type in its ideal formation, in its continuous rebuilding or building anew, has created an autonomous inner world so different and so much its own, that it no longer represents merely a substitute for external reality (original morality) but is something for which reality can offer in every case only a feeble substitute so that the individual must seek satisfaction and release in the creation and projection of a world of his own. In a word, with this type, from all the accepted, the obligatory, from all the wished for, and the willed, from all the aspirations and the commandments is formed neither a compromise, nor merely a summation but a newly created whole, the strong personality with its autonomous will, which represents the highest creation of the integration of will and spirit.

The first level corresponds to the type of duty-conscious, the second to the type of guilt-conscious and the third level finally to the type of self-conscious individual. We see at once that in these three types, which represent a line of development, the relation to reality and to the fellow man is different. The first level is oriented to the external world, corresponds to the adaptation of the ego to it; in this the individual takes over the social and sexual ideals of the majority for his own, and this is not only a passive identification but an effort of will which certainly ends in a submission of will. On the third ethical level there are no longer the external demands or norms, but the own inner ideals, which were not only created by the individual out of himself but which the self also willingly affirms as its own commandments. The second neurotic level represents the failure in going from the first to the third stage; the individual perceives the external commands and norms as compulsion which he must continually oppose, but cannot affirm the ideals which correspond to his own self. Therefore he has guilt feeling toward society (or the various representatives of it) and consciousness of guilt toward himself.

In other words, the first type accepts reality with its demands and so adjusts his own individuality that he perceives and can accept himself as part of reality. He removes the painful feeling of difference since he feels himself one with reality. The third type, on the contrary, accepts himself and his inner ideal formation and seeks accordingly to adjust the environment and the fellow man to himself. This can take place violently as with thoughtless men of action or by way of a reformative ideology, whether it be educational or therapeutic, in the scientific or religious sense of the word. It can, however, also be creative and reaches then its highest level when the individual creates from himself and his own idealized will power, a world for himself, as the artist or the philosopher does, without wanting to force it on others. Certainly this peculiarly creative type also strives for recognition but it cannot, as with the therapeutic reformative personality, be through force or violence, but rather must be the expression of a spontaneous movement of the individual who finds in the creator something related to himself. This creative type finds recognition in himself as he also finds in himself motivation and its approbation

The first adapted type, therefore, needs the external compulsion, the second neurotic type defends itself against every kind of external or internal compulsion, the third creative type has overcome compulsion through freedom. The first type is dependent on reality, the second defends itself against the compulsion of reality, the third creates for itself against the compulsion a reality of its own which makes it independent, but at the same time enables it to live in reality without falling into conflict with it. The second neurotic type is the most interesting psychologically, because it shows that the whole problem at bottom turns on the acceptance of the own individuality on which the attitude toward reality primarily depends. For the neurotic shatters not only on the incapacity to bear external pressure, but he suffers just as much, yes, even more, from the inability to subject himself to any pressure whether it be inside or out, even the pressure of his own ideal formation. The essential therapeutic problem is not, therefore, to adjust him to reality, to teach him to bear external pressure, but to adjust him to himself, that is, to enable him to bear and to accept himself instead of constantly defending himself against himself. If one attains this therapeutic goal, that the individual accepts himself, that is psychologically speaking, that he affirms instead of denies his will, there follows thereupon spontaneously without further effort the necessary adaptation to reality. This, however, cannot form an equally valid scheme for all men, regardless of whether one defines it with the concept of the Œdipus complex like Freud, or again as social feeling like Adler, or as a collective union like Jung. Adaptation ensues with each individual in a different, even in an individual way, from the three possibilities we have described as types. Psychologically speaking, adaptation on the basis of self acceptance may be an acceptance of external norms which finally represents a justification of will, but at least a generally recognized one, or the self acceptance enables the individual to continue his development on the basis of his own ideal formation and its essential difference. In each case, however, the neurotic self denial as it follows from the denial of will must first be overcome constructively in a therapeutic experience.

How this happens I am describing simultaneously in another book.[1] Here I would only like to point out how, as a matter of fact, the various reactions of the individual only correspond to various attitudes to the same fundamental problem. The average man adapted to reality finds the justification of his individual will in the similarly adjusted wills of the majority, but accepts therewith also the universal attempts at justification and unburdening, as society itself apparently uses them in its moral norms and religious projections. The neurotic who in consequence of his stronger individualization feels himself so very different from others, can accept neither the general norms nor the justifications, but neither can he accept his own because they would be an expression of his own will, which he would therewith have to accept. The creative type, on the other hand, accepts as we have said, himself and his ideal, that is, his own individual will, at all events in higher degree than any other type. Certainly he also needs all kinds of external justifications but these work destructively only in the field of intellectual production, like philosophy and science, where they lead to theoretical denial of

[1] See "Will Therapy," Books I and II. Alfred A. Knopf, 1936.

will and justifications which appear under the guise of truth.

This leads us back from the problem of will to the problem of consciousness and conscious knowledge. Where ideal formation works constructively and creatively, it is on the basis of acceptance of the self, of the individual will, which is justified in its own ideal, that is ethically, not morally in terms of the average ideal as with the adapted type. In other words, in its own ideal the originally denied will of the individual manifests itself as ethically justified. The neurotic suffers not only from the fact that he cannot accomplish this, but also from insight regarding it which, according to the degree of insight, manifests itself as consciousness of guilt or inferiority feeling. He rejects the self because in him the self is expressed on the whole negatively as counter-will and accordingly cannot justify itself ethically, that is, cannot reform and revalue itself in terms of an ideal formation. Accordingly he strives only this far, to be himself (as so many neurotics express it) instead of striving to live in accordance with his own ideal. Therefore while the ideal of the average is to be as the others are, the ideal of the neurotic is to be himself, that is, what he himself is and not as others want him to be. The ideal of the creative personality finally is an actual ideal, which leads him to become that which he himself would like to be.

In the sphere of consciousness we see these various levels of development toward ideal formation comprehended in three formulae which correspond to three different ages, world views and human types. The first is the Apollonian, know thyself; the second the Dionysian, be thyself; the third the Critique of Reason, "determine thyself from thyself" (Kant). The first rests on likeness to others and leads in the sense of the Greek mentality to the acceptance of the universal ideal; it contains implicitly the morality, consciously worked out by Socrates, which still lies at the basis of psychoanalytic therapy: know thyself, in order to improve thyself (in the terms of universal norms). It is therefore not knowledge for the sake of the self, but knowledge for the goal of adaptation. The second principle in contrast to the first repudiates likeness and the improvement based on it, as it demands the acceptance of what one is anyway. In contrast to the principle of the Delphic Apollo, I have designated it as Dionysian because, in contrast to adaptation, it leads to ecstatic-orgiastic destruction, as not only Greek mythology but also Ibsen shows in Peer Gynt, who on the basis of the same principle landed in a mad house. The true self, if it is unchained in Dionysian fashion, is not only anti-social, but also unethical and therefore the human being goes to pieces on it. In this sense the longing of the neurotic to be himself is a form of the affirmation of his neurosis, perhaps the only form in which he can affirm himself. He is, as it were, already himself, at any rate far more than the others and has only a step to take in order to become wholly himself, that is, insane. Here comes in the Kantian "Determine thyself from thyself" in the sense of a true self knowledge and simultaneously an actual self creation as the first constructive placing of the problem. Herein lies Kant's historical significance as epistemologist and ethicist. He is indebted to us for the psychology but also a part of his greatness lies therein, for the avoidance of psychologizing has protected him from falling into all the denials, rationalizations and interpretations which form the contents of most psychological theories including the Freudian.

An epistemological psychology without flaw, that is, neither moral nor religious as the Freudian system still is, must start at the point where Kant placed the problem. How can the individual determine himself from himself, or better, why does he do this with such difficulty? Here we strike the will-guilt problem, the knowledge of which remains the indisputable psychological contribution of Schopenhauer. But he has denied the will, while Nietzsche sought to deny the guilt feeling. Freud, finally has seen the guilt problem, as the neurotic presented it to him it is true, but he has tried to solve it by leading it back to a definite content of willing, namely the sexual, while the other analytic schools (Jung, Adler, etc.) differentiate themselves in this, that they have put another content in place of the sexual, and so have hidden the purely psychological will problem itself. The Freudian content disguises itself under the occidental religious morality from which we still suffer and in its failure to solve his individual problem, the modern man has finally shattered in terms of the neurosis.

VI

CREATION AND GUILT

> "Fate sends individuality back to its limitations and destroys it if it transcends them."
> —HEGEL

WE HAVE traced the evolution of the will conflict in the individual from the negative externalization of will, which leads to denial and guilt consciousness to the positive creative power of will, which not only affirms the obligatory instead of denying it, but leads beyond it to a constructive "ought." This "ought" as we have pictured it in the ideal formation of the individual, if the will is able to affirm itself and its own activity on this ethical level, can finally lead to creativity that alters, reforms and builds anew the outer and inner environment as the individual wills it. From the purely psychological act of willing, we have arrived at the moralistic problem of content, that is, what the individual does will or ought to will. The will projection itself, as reaction to an outer or inner counter-will, is independent of the content of the willed. It is related to the "musts" and the "won'ts" as such and accordingly, can have to do even with something that the individual himself has wanted, but does not any more when it is forced on him by a strange will or merely offered, that is, permitted. Apparently it is generally the content itself, a definite content, which the originally denying force of will transforms into a positive, constructive, and finally a creative one with which not only the content of willing in the sense of the own ethical ideal is justified, but also the individual will as such.

Whence comes the content of willing and what does it contain? Just as willing itself arises as an inner, primarily negative opposing force against a compulsion, so the content of willing arises primarily from rejection; we want what we cannot have, that which is denied us. If this first level of willing is determined more negatively from without, so the next level is equally influenced from without, but in terms of desire which already contains a definite willing. We want at that level what others have or want, and this manifests itself as envy or competition in terms of the desire for possessions. But a truly positive willing is arrived at only when we have made this willing our own, that is, have given up comparisons [1] and no longer measure our individual willing by external obstacles or models, but by our own ethical ideal formation. In other words, the will becomes positive, constructive in the ethical justification of the ideal formation and eventually creative from the purely inner will conflict which ensues between the content of our willing and the self ideal of the "ought." If even in this stage the will remains too dependent on outer likeness and justifications in relation to other individuals, there result the feelings of inferiority or guilt which we have comprehended as the neurotic opposite for creative affirmation of will on the ethical level. Before we can understand this in its own terms as the proper subject of this chapter we must first review again the neurotic development.

We must remember that the deeply rooted psychological turning from the affirmation of willing to the denial of the will is closely tied up with the problem of content. All external restrictions and refusals meet the individual in childhood (and also later in life) not as a universal prohibition against willing in general, but as prohibition against willing some definite thing at a certain moment, and are therefore determined in terms of content and eventually also in terms of time. The individual himself, on the contrary, very early connects these particular prohibitions with willing as such. Here it seems to me, as we have noted before, lie the roots of the most important difference and the deepest misunderstanding between the grown-up and the child. In this sense one could say that the child is more ethical than the grown-up average man who is able to think in moralistic concepts only, that is, in terms of content, while for the more impulsive child every restriction, refusal, or prohibition affects the whole of willing, the will as such, and on that account, as we see, is taken so tragically. Briefly put, the momentary content has only symbolic meaning originally, but gradually because of the individual's tendencies to justification, takes on an ever more

[1] See "Will Therapy," Book I, chap. v.

"real" meaning, while the universal impulse life, which is always the essential, is made ever more abstract. Thus the child deceives the adults about willing itself in terms of their own ideology by means of a "good" acceptable content. And equally in the same way, or much more, the adult deceives himself later about the evil of willing itself by means of a content approved by his own ideal or by that of his fellow men. As long as we must justify the evil of willing in terms of its content, so long we feel ourselves morally answerable to others and are accordingly dependent on their praise and blame all the more, the more we are slaves to this deception and self-deception. In the degree, however, that we become conscious of the will itself in its original form of counterwill, as the source of our conflicts with the external world and ourselves, to the same degree do we feel the responsibility with which our own ethical consciousness has to say "Yes" or "No" to our individual willing. And only in this sense can we understand what we now wish to handle as creation but also only in this ethical sense can we comprehend the guilt indissolubly bound up with it not as guilt feeling toward others (in the moralistic sense), also not as consciousness of guilt toward itself (in the neurotic sense), but as guilt in itself, in the ethical sense.

Since we conceive of the creative urge as the expression of will by which willing itself is justified ethically and its content morally, that is, through others, the genesis of the guilt inherent in the creative is to be understood in the following way. The individual seeks to justify his willing in the manner described above, through its "good" content, hence the will branded as bad through the moralistic critique of the content attaches itself to the bad, illicit contents, which are identified from then on with the forbidden will itself. This expresses itself in the child in socalled "being bad," in the adult in the phantasies or day dreams which according to Freud form not only the preliminary step to the neurotic symptoms, but also to creative activity, with both, only insofar and because they represent the aforesaid acts of will which embrace various and, for the most part, forbidden contents. Whether they manifest themselves neurotically or creatively does not depend on content which can be the same in both cases, and is also not to be explained in the Freudian sense by repression, no, not even by the quality and degree of the repression, but seems to me determined only by the relation of the will to the content of willing. In other words, if the good contents of willing are shown and expressed because they imply a moral recognition of will, but the bad are hidden and kept secret because they contain moral condemnation of willing, then their final fate and that of the individual depends on the relation to the will itself, independent of all contents. If the will itself, as pointed out before, is identified with the evil contents and remains so, then these phantasies with the forbidden will content remain secret, that is, the will itself remains evil, condemned, forbidden, in a word, negative counter-will which leads then to repression, denial and rationalization. On the contrary, if the will itself is originally very strong in the individual (as counter-will) then the good contents are not sufficient for the justification of the badness of the will and the individual affirms the forbidden contents also, that is, the bad will itself which they represent. The phantasies are then released from the sphere of mental will expression into the sphere of action, that is, they are no longer kept secret as forbidden, but are transformed into deed as will expression which in this sense is creative. It is not only affirmation of the content stigmatized as evil, but of the individual will which it represents.

The morally proscribed contents themselves are associated originally with the bodily functions. The child must learn to eat and to control the excretory functions, when the adults wish, not when he wishes. His counter-will in relation to this is commonly designated as "bad" and "hateful," but this means restricted and eventually punished. Very soon also the physical expressions of sexuality are drawn in and then become the most important contents of willing, perhaps just because these expressions are so violently put under and forbidden. With regard to the overwhelming part that the psychic plays in our love life, which we will discuss later, the moral prohibition of the physical expression of sex in childhood, has perhaps the biologically valuable effect of strengthening the physical side in its later reaction so that it can stand against the psychic in general. Possibly we have here the ground for that separation of sensuality and tenderness which Freud has described as characteristic of the neurotic, but which I would characterize rather as the attitude of the average, at all events, as more wholesome than the indissoluble union of sensuality with the spiritual which seeks in love the individual justification of sexuality. Again we see here the separation of will from content lying at the root of these phenomena. The tender expressions of love toward certain persons are permitted to the child, are good; the purely physical element of the will is evil, bad.

We said before that the child with the evil forbidden content turns to wish, to phantasy. It seems wholly in accord with my conception that the phantasies of men (of the child as of the adult) relate not so much to the satisfaction of actually forbidden bad contents as to the carrying through of will in itself. To speak bromidically, they are overwhelmingly egoistic even when their content is on a sexual theme. They show the ego of the individual putting through his own will successfully, victoriously against all obstacles. The development into the productive, the creative, represents only a step further in this direction, namely the lifting out of these expressions of will, from the sphere of thought to action. The phantasies are objectified in work, and thus the forbidden content is accomplished somehow, but in the last analysis it is the will expression afforded by creativity, the putting out, the affirmation, that constitutes the satisfying, many times rewarding factor.

Herein lies the essential difference between the average man who keeps the phantasies secret from others, the neurotic who keeps them secret from himself (represses them), and the creative type who affirms them for himself and reveals them to the world, yes, is compelled to do just that. This difference is explained by the different attitudes of the individual to will itself on the one side and to its contents, good or bad, on the other, and this also creates the guilt problem in its various forms. The average man who hides from others the content of the phantasies as an expression of evil will, has guilt feeling (toward the others); the individual who hides them from himself, that is represses them, tries to deny thereby not so much the evil contents as the evil will they represent, has consciousness of guilt (toward himself). Finally the individual who maintains the phantasies and therewith affirms his individual will so that he can transform it into positive action has guilt, makes himself guilty by the individual nature of his doing. Actually guilt arises toward others to whom he opposes himself through his individualization, but also there is guilt toward himself which persists in the justification of this individual will expression. The creative type must constantly make good his continuous will expression and will accomplishment and he pays for this guilt toward others and himself with work which he gives to the others and which justifies him to himself. Therefore he is productive, he accomplishes something because he has real guilt to pay for, not imaginary guilt like the neurotic, who only behaves as if he were guilty but whose consciousness of guilt is only an expression of his will denial, not of creative accomplishment of will which makes one truly guilty.

We notice here that creation and guilt in the ethical sphere present the same contrast as truth and reality in the sphere of knowledge, and that they belong together just as indissolubly. The individually created, the work, is to be generally recognized like truth, and guilt opposes itself to this inhibitingly but also stimulatingly as inner reality, which is continuously overcome by new and ever more lofty feats of will. Accordingly we have to do here with guilt-laden creation and with creative guilt, which in contrast to the more than individual guilt consciousness of the neurotic type, has something specifically personal, individual. What we have here is just the activity of the creative type, not a sublimation of sex instinct, but, on the contrary, the expression of individual will which is almost to be called antisexual. For the authentic creative force proceeds always only from the inner will conflict, as we have described it before, that is, beyond the conflict between ego and sexuality, which the will wages on that level, and with the weapons belonging to that level. It may well be the biologically basic instinct that, in the last analysis, is used as I have already shown in "Der Künstler," but it *is* used. For it creates in the service of the will to its own downfall and what it helps to create is essentially different from itself, in the ideal case, far surpasses it. This is the mighty wrestling between nature and spirit, force and will, which Freud sought to describe with the educational concept of sublimation without recognizing the fundamental difference that lies between reproduction and production, begetting and creating, tool and master, creature and creator.

We recognize therefore in the creative impulse not only the highest form of the will affirmation of the individual, but also the most mighty will conquest, that of the individual will over the will of the species represented by sexuality. A similar victory of the individual will over generic will, as I show elsewhere, is represented in the individual love claim,[1] whose psychological meaning lies in the fact that the individual can and will accept his generic role only if this is possible in an individual personal way, in the love experience. This represents, as it were, the creativity of the average type who demands a definite individuality for himself and if necessary also creates it,[2] an individuality that sanctions and so justifies and saves his individual will. The creative type on the contrary does not content himself with the creation of an individual. Instead he creates a whole world in his own image, and then needs the whole world to say "yes" to his creation, that is, to find it good and thus justify it.

In this sense, to create means to make the inner into outer, spiritual truth into reality, the ego into the world. Biological creating also represents an ego extension in the child, as the love creation represents a confirmation of ego in the "other," but above all the spiritual psychic creation is a creation by itself in the work, the ego is opposed to the world and rules it thus in terms of its will. This manifestation of the ego will in the creation of the work is therefore not a substitute for sexuality and love, but rather both of them are attempts to occupy the creative drive really, attempts which with the creative type always result unsatisfyingly because they always represent forms of expression of the individual creative urge limited by alien counter-wills and accordingly insufficient. Moreover, creativity is not something which happens but once, it is the constant continuing expression of the individual will accomplishment, by means of which the individual seeks to overcome self-creatively the biological compulsion of the sexual instinct and the psychological compulsion to emotional surrender.

[1] See the corresponding conclusions in Chapter V of "Will Therapy."
[2] On the projective creation of the love object compare "Verliebheit und Projektion" in "Genetische Psychologie," Part II.

This conception of the creative will as a victory of the individual over the biological sexual instinct explains the guilt which the development and affirmation of the creative personality necessarily produces. It is this going beyond the limits set by nature as manifested in the will accomplishment to which the ego reacts with guilt. Only this guilt reaction makes completely intelligible the projection of the God idea by means of which the individual again subjects himself to a higher power. For the primitives who spiritualized the world, this was nature itself, for heroic man triumphing over nature it was the creative God made by himself, therefore his own will at once glorified, denied and justified, and finally for the man of our western culture, it is the really fateful powers of parental authority and love choice, to which he wishes to submit voluntarily, that is, ethically.

This entire conflict complex we find represented on a grand scale in the myth of the fall of man, which presents the level of knowledge on which consciousness wants to control and rule sexuality, that is, to use it for its own pleasure and satisfaction. The hero Adam is not punished because he exults in his Godlike knowledge, but because he wants to use it to force the sex instinct into the service of his individual will. It is not the father complex that can give us understanding here, as little as can the contrasting Greek figure Prometheus. It is just the reverse. The utilization of the sexual instinct in the service of the individual will on the basis of knowledge of good and evil, that is, the affirmation of the evil willing, brings suffering and punishment. The punishment consists in the loss of paradisical naïveté, of oneness with nature and her laws, and the recently won order among them. Adam is punished for not wanting to become a father and the punishment is the obligation to become one, that is, subordination under the compulsion of the biological sexual drive, in spite of knowledge of the moral problem which has branded the pleasure will as evil, and the attempt to overcome this morality through will affirmation.

The hero becomes thus the psychological representative of the creative man whose negative opposite we see before us in the neurotic type. The hero does not disown the parents in the sense of the Œdipus complex, that is, because he wants to put himself in the father's place, but because he is the earthly representative of God, that is, of the creative will. Accordingly he has no children (which he would have to in the role of father) but expresses himself and his individual will in works, in heroic deeds. He knows no gratitude (toward parents) and no guilt feeling (toward others), but he has guilt which derives from creating. Not that the fact that he wants to become the father or to be God gives him guilt consciousness, but that he is God, that he occupies himself creatively, makes him guilty and this guilt can only be atoned for through further performance and finally through death. I believe moreover that the idea of hero formation, as explained in the material presented in the "Myth of the Birth of the Hero" was strongly influenced by the discovery of the man's share in procreation. At all events the conscious comprehension of the male process of procreation seems to signify a revolutionary turning point in the history of mankind.

A whole area of will and guilt psychology as the present day neurotic still shows, seems to me to be grounded in the fact that man on the one hand could feel himself as a creator who creates human beings (Prometheus), on the other hand could control this biological procreative act consciously and thus utilize sexuality for mere pleasure gain (Adam's knowledge?). Moreover, the discovery of this connection gave the first real basis for the social and psychological father concept, against whose recognition the individual defends himself even in the myth of the hero with the denial of the father and the emphasis on the maternal role. Here is to be found perhaps a powerful motive for the fact that God representing the individual ego-will took on fatherly features at a certain period. The autonomous heroic individual could not endure and use the biological dependence on an earthly progenitor and ascribed it all the more readily to the already installed creator God who received in this way paternal features, which give psychological expression to the hero's self creation.

Moreover the first intimation of the individual love problem betrays itself here in the creation of the woman from the man and in his own image. Here the woman is a product of the creative man, who ascribes to himself this divine creative power and divine knowledge—like the Greek Prometheus. We recognize therein the first faint beginnings of that magnificent process of rivaling the Gods which we have understood psychologically as the gradual acknowledgment of the conscious individual will in the human being. It appears in a glorious fashion in Greek culture with the heroes rebelling against the Gods, and reaches the peak of its development in Christianity with the humanizing of God and the deifying of man. If man had first to manifest his own creative will in the formation of God, but at the same time had to justify it, so in the heroic period, at the other extreme, he fell into the deification of himself, of his own individual will in order finally to deify and worship in the individual love experience, the other individual who represents the creation and redemption of his own individual will. Christianity as the religion of love and guilt unites all the conflicting elements of this will-guilt problem in itself. It shows us in the humanizing of God, the continuation of "heaven" on earth. It is still in the form of universal brotherhood as it also led away from individualism, for it created a mass hero of such great sweep that every man could feel himself redeemed in and through him.

Our whole spiritual development is thus represented by the three levels, the Jewish, the Greek and the Christian, which represent not only historical phases, but also psychological types, ways of reacting and attitudes even of modern men. They correspond to the different attempts to solve the will-guilt problem, the real, the ideal and the spiritual. The biblical Jews were a rough, warlike nation of herdsmen who needed and created a strong willed, confident god of battle as an ego ideal. If one understands "Jahwe" as the personification of the hard and tenacious individual will of the wild herdsman constantly fighting against enemies, then one recognizes in the Bible the first noble attempt of a victorious people arrived at stability and prosperity to dethrone their old god of war and to perceive themselves in his strong will. But after that, all that is accomplished and attained is ascribed to a creative God who earlier had only been a destructive one, and to whom the chosen people which feels itself as completely heroic, voluntarily submits. Thus the warlike Jewish people first sought their leader, embodied in the hero Moses, in a strong willed God, as later they sought in him the justification for all the horrors and conquests of war.

Also the Greeks originally had to fight hard for their existence and the few fertile spots open to them as the Iliad shows. Their reaction to final victory and prosperity was no late justification through the creation of an individual God, but an increase in the affirmation of individual self-feeling as we understand it in the myths of the heroes. No longer do the gods cause and guide war and the battles of heroes, but world happenings are influenced by the super-human passions, the strong wills of the heroes, who perish through their own passions, therefore of their own will. Only much later there enters here as reaction to this creative arrogance the hybrid, the creeping poison of consciousness of guilt, which we see the tragic poets transfer to the heroes themselves instead of ascribing it to the gods. In this sense Greek civilization actually represents the birth of individuality in human history. Man himself takes the place of God in the form of the self-ruling creative hero, a God whose first twilight appears here in his passive role of spectator. Accordingly also we have the excessive guilt feeling of the Greeks as it manifests itself particularly in tragedy as a reaction to the heroic phase. In the Greek tragic poet the hero, as it were, makes himself fully responsible for himself and pays, atones, with death.

Here lies their difference from the Jewish nation, which could keep and preserve the fruits of victory because they put the responsibility for it back on God. The Greek who recognized and acknowledged deed and guilt equally as an expression of his individual will came to grief in the tragic recognition of the will problem and self responsibility while the Jew converted the evil, destroying, recognition "therapeutically" into the moral compulsion of good and evil and made it concrete in a meaningful will prohibition, the decalogue, which protected him from stepping over the boundaries set for the individual will. Christianity, as an immediate reaction to Roman tyranny, representing paternal authority, presents in the symbolism of the rebellious son, the passive hero, who conquers, not by means of will assertion but by means of will submission, conquers spiritually even though corporeally, physically, he fails. Therewith the struggle is lifted from the sphere of the real to the unreal, while Greek culture had lifted it from the moral to the ethical. At the same time, in Christianity God is brought from the unreal sphere to the real, just as with the Greek heroes, only still further humanized, as it were, made into a universal hero. In this sense Christianity is a reaction to and attempt at healing from the danger of individualism, as it had culminated in terms of will in the Roman autocratic system of father rule. If, therefore, the creative God was the strongest expression of the individual ego will, so the mild, forgiving God of the Christian faith is the strongest expression of the self depreciatory ego which presents itself in terms of the Roman ideology as son, that is, as creature and not as creator. Therewith at the same time, it tries to reprimand the father as creator and lifts the mother principle to a spiritual significance which it had not had formerly. Here the realization of the will principle as we see it in the Roman father rule begins to oppose the realization of the maternal love principle, which reaches its height in the individual love claim and love creation of the modern irreligious man.

Thus the hero formation emphasizes the divine in man, affirms, glorifies the individual creative power of will while religion formation seeks to deny it and shows man again as the creature who humbly subjects himself to the higher racial will. In this sense the Jews represent the religious; the Greeks the heroic; and Christianity the human solution of the will-guilt problem. The first is moralistic, the second ethical, the third spiritual. This is associated with the transformation of the guilt problem which again is dependent on the level of consciousness. With the Jews, God represents the will and the individual the guilt; with the Greeks the individual hero represents will and guilt; in Christianity God represents guilt and the individual subjects his will to the God conquered and overcome by himself. In the same degree that we see the will in the individual develop and then break, we can substantiate an analogous displacement and denial in the sphere of consciousness; with the Jews recognition of the moralistic solution as the saving of the individual; with the Greeks recognition of the ethical problem as the fall of the individual; in Christianity the recognition of the human problem as the abrogation of the individual, as release from the compulsion of the will and the torment of the conscious responsibility as creator. Accordingly Christianity puts the emotional experience of love in the center and brings the female principle again into a position of honor, in its symbolic meaning; the Greek puts the creative principle first, which leads to guilt, and therewith brings

73

forward the individual artist, while the Jews represent the will
principle and therewith paternal compulsion. Accordingly,
force, freedom and love represent different reactions (by Jews,
Greeks and Christians) to the will-guilt problem. Thus each of
these culture groups represents a certain level of development
of the will-guilt problem as it manifests itself in the individual
also; the Jew, the conscious recognition of the paternal compulsion principle of morality; the Greek, the creative recognition of the heroic principle of freedom; the Christian, the recognition of suffering, of the maternal love principle.

With this advance from divine projection to human justification of the individual will, the part of consciousness, especially
in the developing recognition of self consciousness, is of decisive
importance. The first level, the projection of deity, presents as
yet no conscious creating, rather an attempt to transfer the will
expression represented in the wish phantasy in a magic form and
way, to a personified ego whose will and counter-will correspond
to the own will. In the active hero, who converts his conscious will
into the deed, we glimpse the first recognition of the individual
forming and reforming reality in accordance with his personal
desires, who, however, like Œdipus, is destroyed as soon as he
perceives his little human truth. Through increasing self consciousness, therefore, the whole mechanism of will projection
with simultaneous denial of willing, like will expression with
simultaneous denial of knowledge, is dethroned, humanized, re-
moved from God to man, from heaven to earth. It continues,
however, on the earth, and in truth, in the love experience, and
in the love relation, which again in the last analysis only represents an attempt to put the responsibility for our will and counter-will upon another, whom we make into a divinity and against
whose will we revolt at the same time if it does not resemble our
own and bow to it. Here, in the love relationship, in the recrea-
tion of the other after our own image, we again come up against
the real counter-will of the other which we have evaded in such
a cunning fashion in the creation of a God, for the divine will
represented our own will and at the same time justified it.

Only in our occidental culture has God become creative, not
merely conserving like the ancient Godheads who were themselves
creatures, like their creators of that period, the ancients. This

creative God, as the occidental systems of religion have evolved him, is not any longer mere projection but is himself a creative expression of the individual will, not just a father who does not create but only begets. This creative, omnipotent, omniscient God is the first great manifestation of the individual will, at the same time its denial and justification in the supra-individual world will, nature. The creation of God ensues cosmically, not in imitation of the dependence on parents which corresponds to a much later interpretation on a certain level of family organiza- tion. On the other hand, the primitive God who existed before the creative one was dangerous and destroying, a manifestation of the evil counter-will which, in the later systems, was ascribed to a negative deity, as we know it from Ahriman to the Christian "devil." Against this original, destructive, hostile God, who is still preserved in the creator Jahwe, were gradually called upon for help, protective deities, who bore the maternal character, as for example, the Egyptian and even Athena in the Homeric world picture. The image of the creative God, as the highest de- velopmental level of this ethical process, proceeds then from an overcoming of the evil counter-will to its affirmation in creative willing, but carries in addition the maternal conservative char- acteristics of preserving and protecting that which he creates. Only later and under the influence of our present and still per- sistent family and social organization and in the service of its maintenance does God take on strong paternal characteristics, which correspond more to the external counter-will of the stronger than to the individual creative will. In this father God, who actually corresponds to a reduced, degenerate God of will, the individual grown equally proud in the spheres of will and consciousness, sets upon earth a strong real counter-will, which shall again keep within bounds the individual who demands for himself the divine power of will.

Perhaps the predominance of the father principle itself whose culmination in the Roman state was broken by Christianity, is to be understood psychologically just from the fact that the "father" represents the strong willed man who dares to ascribe to himself the divine prerogative and whose domination is ac- cepted not only on the basis of force, but equally from the neces- sity of placing other earthly bounds to the all powerful will of the ego which is always being put further back into the individual. It would be the psychological opposite of our conception of love as a humanizing of the self deifying tendency, since the father principle in its proper and psychological manifestations would correspond to a humanization of the negative side of will, of the counter-will. Be that as it may, at all events, for us the opposition of the mother and father principle as it has come to expression recently in the contrast of Bachhofen's world view to that of Haller [1] and in the various psychoanalytic interpretations, corresponds to the opposition between natural right and forced right, in other words between love and force, or psychologically speaking, between the positive will (mother) and counter-will (father). In other words, the father represents, as I have said before, only a symbol of the own actually inhibited will, but not the creative power of will as it is presented in the occidental God, creator of heaven and earth. Freud takes part in this denying rationalizing attempt of guilt conscious humanity in his theory, where, as it were, the individual will hides itself behind the father principle; hides in a double sense, quite as in the creation of God, for the father symbolizes the own will but the individual hypocritically denies his own will which he ascribes to the father in order to be able to subordinate himself to it. In this humble subordination of the weak helpless creature to the parental will, psychoanalysis is religious, in its actual domination of consciousness it is presumptuously heroic. That means that the analyst must pay for his likeness to God in knowledge and in creation (re-creation) of men, since he must represent the individual as such, including himself, as an unfree, powerless creature who, a pawn of his unconscious wishes and evil impulses, has lapsed into guilt.

This is not intended to be an attempt to present a psychoanalysis of Freud as, for example, Michaelis has recently undertaken, but it is a psychology of the creative man who must always be denying his godlike power of will in order to unburden himself of the creative guilt. Again we see how the special and the individual can only be understood on the grounds of the universal not the reverse. Just as the father concept in the social sense only

[1] Bachhofen: Selbstbiographie und Antrittsrede über das Naturrecht. Edited and introduced by Alfred Bäumler, Halle 1927.

represents the earthly personification of the own consciousness of will, so also the Œdipus complex is only a special instance of cosmic fate in which man wants to free himself from dependence on natural forces, and yet cannot deny his littleness and helplessness in the face of the universe. But the Œdipus complex is also a special case in another sense. For the child of our modern social organization, probably the parents represent the first will forces, as it were, his world, his cosmos, and this remains the incontestable psychological meaning of the parent relation. Very soon, however, the child grows beyond these family symbols of the will conflict to the perception of his own inner will conflict which soon goes beyond the external one in intensity and meaning. For the primitive man, on the other hand, nature itself which we now rule with our wills to a large extent, was the threatening external will power against which he found himself helpless and which he learned to fight and to rule with his will. Here is the place to seek the origin of all threatening and terrifying Gods and spirits who show their evil influence even deep within the Greek heroic world and against which they called upon maternal protective deities for aid. These, however, had a far more cosmic than feminine significance, that is, they called to their aid the conserving and preserving powers of nature against the evil destructive natural forces. For regardless of what one calls the cosmic preserving principle, the biologically dependent child of man understands it through the image of the mother while the father as symbol of will power not only emerges much later, but also belongs to a wholly different psychological plane, namely the sphere of conscious will.

Accordingly the evolution of the God concept moves from the personification of natural forces threatening the helpless and defenseless individual to the conserving maternal principle, under whose protection the individual first arrives at the strengthening and unfolding of his own will. The self representation of the same we see in the creative God, who represents the omnipotence of conscious will much more than the domination of the father whose biological procreative rule and whose social ascendancy lie as far from childish thinking as from primitive. The next and psychologically most interesting developmental level is characterized by the guilt concept attached to the creative God idea, which was lacking on the earlier level, because fear was then the driving force. The creative God corresponds to one side of the self representation of the conscious will power of the individual, but is at the same time an attempt at its denial and the throwing off of responsibility, and leads accordingly to creative guilt, which belongs to the will expression as such, manifested in the creation of God himself. We get here, from the understanding of the creation of the creative God, a glimpse into the psychology of a creator, of the occidental individual and his guilt problem ensuing from the individual will. This understanding continues into the further development of the modern individual and his relation to the God concept, which concerns chiefly the guilt problem from which we suffer, henceforth individually with a growing conscious knowledge of this whole connection, so that no general salvation but only the individual happiness of each separate person seems the solution.

The psychic process of dissolution in which we now find ourselves and as the extensive neurotic type represents it, concerns not only the knowledge of the God creation as a projection and justification of the individual will, but extends to the real representatives of this will conflict, the moralistic parent authorities in the social sphere and the releasing love objects in the sexual. We see here again how progress in knowledge hinders experiencing, in other words, how self consciousness inhibits will projection, for the creation of the creative God was not only a manifestation and an expression of the creative individual will, but made possible to the individual at the same time in its justification tendency, creative action on earth. In truth it all happened in the service of religion, to the glory of God, but at least it did happen. All the creative powers of the individual, both of an artistic and productive kind could unfold under the justifying symbol of the creative God. This holds for the culture of the middle ages through the church more than for the ancients, where the hero was still the representative of divine will power on earth. With the general humanizing of God, as Christianity initiated it, the hero, the creative man, becomes as it were a universal type, whose development culminates in the modern individualized man, when actually each separate person is himself a God, a personality stamped with a strong will. Now, instead of its leading to heightened creative will activity, as one might expect, we see this strong individualistic will in the neurotic type directed as counter-will against itself and the fellow man and thus denying in itself both itself and its own creative power.

The basis for this is easy to see in the light of what we have just said. With the knowledge and the perception of the divine power of creation as his own individual power of will, the individual must also take over the responsibility for it himself, and this leads necessarily to the ethical guilt concept, which relates to willing itself and not like the moralistic guilt feeling, to any particular content of will. The conscious knowledge of divine creativity leads therefore beyond an heroic phase in which the individual voluntarily takes upon himself and affirms will and responsibility, to a new erection of the rule of God on earth, as we recognized it in the love principle on the one side and in the father principle on the other. Both correspond to current attempts to solve the will conflict in reality, after its magnificent unreal solution in the God concept had been destroyed by the knowing power of consciousness and the disintegrating force of self consciousness. But this twilight of the Gods now approaching its end is accompanied by a still more fatal and tragic process, which one might designate as the disenthroning of the individual himself, the result of which we have before us in the neurotic type with its guilt and inferiority feelings.

For the earthly attempts at justification of the individual will also are shattered by the power of the counter-will only to end finally in a kind of psychological "twilight of the ego," with a tormenting hopelessness of the individual thrown upon his own resources. The basis for this, as has already been pointed out, is that something is lacking in all real attempts at solution of this will conflict which the unreal God creation, whose very faults actually made solution possible, did not have. It is this, the fact that the earthly representatives of the individual ego themselves have an own will and a counter-will against which our own constantly strike. The father or the parental authority represents not only a symbol of the child's own will, but also—and probably equally early and strongly—a strange counter-will, which disturbs and restrains its own. In the love relation, which, as already noted, represents entirely individual creative activity, yes exactly *the* creative activity of the individual as such, he runs against the same counter-will which wants to occupy itself creatively on him. This makes the conflicts of the modern man so difficult and deep because the inner will conflict cannot become released really through an external agent, but apparently is only to be temporarily and partially unburdened in the more suitable manner of unreal projection.

The neurotic human type of our time has therefore not only exploded the God illusion itself, but perceives the real substitute for it as we have recognized it in the parental authority and love objects to be unsatisfying for solving or even lessening the inner will conflict heightened through knowledge and intensified by self consciousness. Knowledge, which we have understood as an intellectual will experience in terms of spiritual truth, leads therefore to taking the Gods from heaven and to the humanizing of the omnipotent creative will. The tormenting self consciousness which again leads to the denial of the individual will thus affirmed, comes into the picture first when the will conflict is thrown back from the real personifications of it as we recognized them in the parent authorities and love objects, through the counter-will, upon the individual himself and this leads to the recognition of his own inner conflicts. However, this throwing back does not ensue as we consciously strive for it in the therapeutic experience, in a constructive fashion so that the individual can accept himself as conflicted, instead the actual conflict only shows the individual that he cannot find salvation from the evil will in the "other" either. The therapeutic value of the analytic situation as such lies in the fact that it affords the individual an unreal solution of his will conflict corresponding to the creation of God from the own will, but at the same time lets him experience in the actual emotional relation to the analyst and understand in this connection the real earthly parallel.

The therapeutic experience is thus only to be understood from the creative experience because it is itself a creative experience and in truth a very special form of it which we describe more fully and make intelligible elsewhere.[1] Just as for the individual neurotic the therapeutic experience represents the last deliverance from the two-fold conflict of the negative denial of will and

[1] See the chapter "Love and Force" in Book I of "Will Therapy."

destructive self consciousness, so the creative type as such is the last salvation of human kind from the same inevitable neurotic conflict which we all work against. The creative man saves himself first of all from the neurotic chaos of will denial and self consciousness since he affirms himself and his own creative will, which at once protects him in the growing advance of consciousness from falling into the inhibiting self consciousness. He keeps for himself the capacity to manifest himself and his individual will creatively instead of denying and reacting to it with guilt consciousness. He expresses himself instead of knowing himself consciously, wills instead of knowing or knows that he wills and what he wills and lives it. His guilt consists in the fact of his release from common pressure, whether it be biological or moral, in his isolation, which however he can affirm creatively instead of having to deny it neurotically. His creativity cancels his guilt while the neurotic willing makes the individual guilt-conscious with its denial. Since he transforms the neurotic self consciousness arising from the hypertrophied compulsive thinking into creative living again, that is, into individual will affirmation, he does isolate himself it is true, as an individual from his contemporaries who suffer from consciousness, but unites them again with positive natural forces, thus revealing at once the grandeur and strength of man.

The creative man is thus first of all his own therapist as which I have already conceived him in "Der Künstler," but at the same time a therapist for other sufferers. Only he solves his individual will conflict in a universal form which does not satisfy the hyperindividualized type of our time. This type needs and desires no longer a common savior, but an individual one; he comes to the therapist, however, as soon as and because he has broken down in the individual therapy which the love experience affords. In analysis he tries again the unreal and real methods of salvation which no longer work for him because for his heightened and hypertrophied self consciousness there is only one savior—and that is himself! In this sense the therapeutic experience, as I pointed out before, is to be understood only from the creative. For in the first place the therapist is a creator, and in truth almost a creative God, and not made so first by the patient. For he creates men in the Promethean sense, men who like himself have the creative will, but must deny it instead of being able to affirm it. And this is the second reason why the therapeutic experience is only to be understood from the creative. For the patient is also a creator, but a miscarried negative one and his powerful identification with the therapist arises from this, that at bottom he is the same and would like to possess creative power positively also. This therapeutic creation of men, which the patient on that account presents as a rebirth experience, cannot ensue on the basis of a general norm or a common ideal for which the neurotic type is just as unsuited as is the creative, and he cannot be educated to it either. The only therapeutic possibility with our modern individual neurotic type is to permit him to develop and accept his own individuality, in other words, to allow the individual to mold himself into that which he is, that is, to affirm his own will and therewith his individuality. This can happen, however, only in an individual personal experience of therapy, where again we meet the guilt bound up with creation, the release of which presents the greatest difficulty for this individual type of therapy.

Since we are keeping these problems for presentation in "Will Therapy," we turn in conclusion to one more universal viewpoint which is important not only for individual therapy, but also for the universal therapy of the creative type. We spoke of different phases and levels of the formation of religion and the creation of God, which certainly have a history, whose interesting evolution and many aspects we have no intention of giving here. These historical allusions are only a convenient help in the presentation of these complicated processes in the individual and serve merely to illustrate the point of view, which seems to me essential to the understanding of the individual structure and its reactions. We spoke of a period of evil deities, of protective gods, of will gods, of father gods, of the deifying of love and finally of self deification in the heroic man as well as of his negative, the self condemnation of the hyperconscious neurotic hemmed in by guilt feeling. All these and yet other phases, developmental levels and reactions we find to vary in the single individual himself at different periods of his development. I do not believe, however, that we are able to understand the historical development in the past through projecting backwards or drawing conclusions a posteriori from the individual. Rather it would perhaps be possible that the past, if we should understand it from its own time, might light up many an individual of the present who seems to be going through similar phases, not only in terms of an ontogenetic repetition of the phylogenetic as it lies at the basis of the Jungian concept of the "collective" unconscious, but from his own will conflict, which, in contact with the outer reality of his fellow men and with the inner reality of his own consciousness and development manifests itself in similar fashion. We are concerned therefore with parallel phenomena as the ancient world picture conceived it in the opposition of microcosm and macrocosm, not with causal connections as they underlie the concept of phylogenesis, whether one undertakes to explain the past from the individual or vice versa wants to understand the individual from the past. For the guilt is no accumulated guilt, neither historical nor individual and all attempts thus to explain it represent a misuse of the natural science principle of causality in the service of will justification. Guilt arises in and from the individual and must continue to produce evil if the individual uses it for the justification of his evil will, when it appears as neurotic guilt consciousness and not as creative guilt which can be atoned for through new creation.

VII

HAPPINESS AND REDEMPTION

> "I drink not from mere joy in wine nor to
> scoff at faith—no, only to forget myself
> for a moment, that only do I want of
> intoxication, that alone."
>
> —OMAR KHAYYAM

AT THIS point we leave the historical and typological methods
of comparison which forced themselves upon us as parallel phenomena in considering creation as a continuous ongoing and developing life process, and return to those spiritual states which
always emerge in the individual as reactions to the will-guilt conflict as we have described it, and influence and determine its manifestations decisively. The longing for happiness and redemption
dwelling in all of us can only be expressed as a momentary present life value for the individual and can only be understood from
that viewpoint. Accordingly we see the need for happiness and
redemption in humankind becoming always more individualized.
Upon the religious justification and the heroic ethical solution of
the will-guilt problem, there follows the effort to find individual
redemption in the emotional love experience, which gives this
developmental phase value not only historically, but also individually for the particular person with whom it characterizes
childhood, puberty and maturity. We need for the understanding
of these parallel phenomena no phylogenetic causality, but only
the will causality of the individual from which the same reactions
always follow ·with psychological necessity. In the course and
progress of the latter we have discovered, in addition to the principle of will causality, another principle derived from it which
has helped determine the gradual transformation of the concepts
of happiness and redemption decisively. This is the "Realisierungsprinzip" [1] which in distinction from the "reality principle"

[1] This term has no suitable equivalent in English. It means a making real,
a literal "realizing" in contradistinction to the static "reality principle."

of Freud has a dynamic significance inasmuch as it views reality, not as something given once and for all to which the individual adapts himself more or less, but as something which has come into being, yes, is continuously becoming.

We have illustrated this principle of the gradual and continuously changing realization of the unreal and the reverse process of making the real unreal which parallels it, in the evolution of the idea of God. This develops in humanity and in the individual from the projection of the most real principle of all, namely, the will, in the unreal concept of God, to the real personification of the counter-will in the father principle, and of positive willing in the love principle. Our scientifically oriented era, however, has driven this "Realisierungsprinzip" still further toward its denial in the moralistic parent ideology, and the ethical love ideology since it would make the spiritual itself real, a last despairing attempt which we see culminate in the psychoanalytic world view. At the same time we see the neurotic type of our time suffering from the loss of all illusions, breaking away from the psychoanalytic therapy which makes the will concrete and justifies the guilt really, and striving after new spiritual experiences, as indicated in parallel attempts toward a new orientation of psychology in terms of total personality and total experience. This reaction of the spiritual against the psychological seems to me to correspond to a reaction against the whole scientific ideology to whose practical consequences and activities man reacts on the one side with guilt, as to all of his will consequences, while on the other he flees to spiritual reality, that is, to emotional experience in order to find there salvation from will as well as from consciousness.

Whatever the need for happiness and salvation may have meant to the men of an earlier age, for the hyperconscious, will-restricted neurotic type of today they represent the attempts to get free of the conscious will-ego temporarily or permanently, in a word, they strive for an abrogation of the individualism from whose isolating consequences we suffer. As always, the man of earlier times sought to win happiness and salvation or to imagine it, while for us, after the failure of the common attempts to make real or unreal as they lie before us in religion and science, there remains only the individual solution carried out in the love experience, whose failure has led finally to the most individualistic form of therapy. Already the hypertrophied self consciousness of the neurotic type begins to recognize this latest illusion of an individual therapy as affording neither happiness nor salvation. This recognition, however, like all psychological knowledge, is no creative one in terms of a pleasurable will affirmation but a painful becoming conscious, a disillusioning awareness of all these connections which we do not will to know for the sake of knowledge, but which we have to know because no other course remains open to us. In order to comprehend this process of decay in all illusions, the unreal as well as the real, in its full bearing, and to understand the inherent need of modern man for redemption, we must examine it, especially in the three aspects which it offers us today, namely, its relation to sexuality, to the emotional life, and to the consciousness of the individual.

In relation to sexuality, we find that the modern man no longer understands and experiences the sexual purely biologically, but as we have explained, uses it morally as the essential content of the will and guilt problem, which inevitably contributes to the formation of the neurotic conflict. From this it follows that he has also attached the need for happiness and redemption to the sexual content, insofar as it is to free him from the compulsion of the moralistic. In other words, having utilized sexuality psychologically, he now wants to use it spiritually. Originally sexuality had as little to do with morality as with redemption, but its original biological meaning does not explain its modern role and function. In its psychological meaning as will accomplishment, which it represents for both sexes, sexuality can probably afford happiness, insofar as happiness is perception of pleasure, that is, a brief consciousness of will accomplishment itself. However it can afford no salvation that aims at the dissolution of, or escape from individuality, from the conscious self, because it is sex that emphasizes difference in the highest degree and accordingly can only be pleasurable, that is, affording happiness, when the individual, man or woman, is able to affirm his individuality and its will. This the neurotic is not able to do and accordingly sexuality affords him not even the happiness of a brief self forgetting but only increases his awareness of difference, that is, increases his guilt consciousness. Sexuality tends to make possible for him a flight from consciousness instead of enjoyment of the will achievement in consciousness, which constitutes the essence of pleasure. Sexuality with this opposition of sex and will becomes the symbol of inner conflict instead of release therefrom. For him this real solution with the freedom of will in the love choice and its justification through the "other" becomes the compulsion of racial will which the "other" represents for the individual will, and to which, accordingly, the counter-will reacts negatively.

The erotic emotional experience lifts these difficulties found in the physical sex relation to a certain level in the releasing happiness of love but shatters on other grounds in the final solution of the conflict as well as in the redemption of the individual from it. In the emotional experience the individual yields primarily through his own emotion, so that the giving up to the other is no subjection of the will actually, but only the consequence of his own voluntary softening of the will. The emotional experience represents therefore a kind of attempt at self redemption which actually aims at independence of the other will and object and also strives not for the other's subjection, but its own subjection. This giving in of will holds for both sexes, exactly as the physical sex act means for both sexes will accomplishment. The conflict re-enters in the emotional sphere when the will opposes the yielding to the other, so that the individual who finds salvation in his own emotional yielding finally strives after redemption from this individual emotional compulsion as he formerly strove after release from the racial sex compulsion in the emotional love experience.

Here again we see that the need of man for happiness and redemption not only changes with different historical and individual developmental phases but that, exactly as does the spiritual content of truth, it varies in terms of the momentary will and guilt picture. From what serves today as a means to salvation, the individual at once, or tomorrow, wants to be saved as soon as this form of salvation becomes compulsory. This situation is most highly complicated in the sphere of consciousness in which, finally, all these conflicts manifest themselves. If consciousness in its original function as the instrument of will affirms the latter's achievement, then it mediates the sensation of pleasure, but the pleasure experience then struggles after rescue from the quality of consciousness, begrudging its momentariness, and seeks to make happiness a salvation. This pleasure, which in Nietzsche's meaning wants eternity, as it struggles loose from time conditioned consciousness becomes pain when consciousness does not affirm the will but denies it and so leads to guilt consciousness instead of consciousness of pleasure. The longing for redemption, then, has to do with guilt consciousness as a tormenting form of self consciousness which originally mediates pleasure through affirmation of the will.

We find ourselves through this discussion in the midst of the whole problem of redemption which, depending on circumstances, is connected with will or consciousness, pleasure or guilt. We notice here also that happiness and redemption, at least as we understand them in the modern individual, actually represent opposites and not merely different degrees of a longing directed toward the dissolution of individuality. For the achievement of happiness represents a peak of individualism and its pleasurable will affirmation through personal consciousness while the longing for salvation, on the contrary, strives after the abrogation of individuality, for likeness, unity, oneness with the all. Accordingly happiness is only to be attained in the will accomplishment, salvation only in the abrogation of will through emotion. But this giving up of will, although it is also pleasurable, is only achieved through guilt feeling from which state redemption is then sought in turn. In this sense, the feeling of happiness releases only temporarily from will compulsion, while what we seek is the actual lasting release from tormenting guilt consciousness.

Here we come upon the time element whose quantitative aspect is not only determining for the feeling of happiness and redemption, but in general represents the central factor of consciousness itself and therewith of spiritual life as such. For all our spiritual tendencies, from whatever standpoint one may view them, can be understood finally like life itself, temporally. With all so-called psychic mechanisms, we have to do ultimately with the shortening or prolonging of psychic states; to shorten to the point of nothingness, as, for example, denial does, or to prolong to infinity as in the belief in immortality. The situation, however, is not so simple as that we merely want to prolong pleasurable conditions and shorten unpleasurable ones; we here strike the paradox that the individual wants to prolong the pleasure whose essence lies just in its temporal limitation, which must miscarry in the same way as the shortening of pain, whose essence lies in the prolongation of any psychic state, even one that is pleasurable in the beginning. For pleasure is a certain brevity of consciousness, pain a lengthening of consciousness, at least on the level of neurotic self consciousness, where consciousness disturbs experience in the form of self consciousness and guilt consciousness and accordingly the individual wants to be saved from it.

Therefore from the standpoint of the psychology of emotions, consciousness shows itself as a time problem in the sense that time represents the form of consciousness and by means of this time factor makes the different contents pleasurable or painful. Will as the constant driving force strives accordingly to prolong its pleasurably perceived affirmation through consciousness, to make the feeling of happiness lasting, that is, redeeming. Insofar as this prolongation succeeds, it is perceived as painful because compulsory and thus the individual wants again to get free of the spirits which he himself has called up. Thus sex pleasure which does away with the inner will conflict pleasurably through realization, is intended to be made lasting through the love emotion; this emotional dependence, however, is perceived as compulsory and the individual strives for release through conscious effort of will which leads to guilt feeling, and from which again salvation is sought in the sphere of unconsciousness. Here belong all ideas of salvation with eternal duration from the Buddhistic Nirvana to the Christian immortality, which, however, only strive after a redemption from tormenting self consciousness and have as little to do with actual biological death as Freud's "death instinct." For the painful reality from which the individual wants to get free is his own consciousness in the form of self consciousness and release is sought in the overcoming of the temporal form of consciousness, that is, in permanence or eternity symbols, for which procreation and death as contents given in the biological process have always been preferred.

Man felt himself immortal as long as he knew nothing of time, as long as he had no time consciousness. This is the meaning of the myth of the fall which represents symbolically this human destiny generally as the guilt of knowledge while the Greek myth attaches the transition from the immortal God to mortal man in almost psychological formulation to the breaking in of time consciousness. Uranos, the eternal God of heaven, is emasculated by Kronos, a symbol of time and temporal duration which from that point on had dominion over the world and men. If Freud had named the basal complex here after the hero instead of the content, he would have recognized in the "Kronos complex" what is perhaps the most important and powerful complex for the modern man. With him the time problem as a psychological determinant enters into human consciousness and its development. The eternal biological principle of procreation which the myth represents cosmically in the love union of heaven with earth, breaks through in human self consciousness in the form of time consciousness. From then on human ideas of salvation take on the character of eternity which culminates in the blessed life of the Christian kingdom of heaven. The psychological recognition of the time problem as the form of human consciousness, therefore, leads away from the brief instinct satisfaction of happiness, to the eternal lasting peace of blessedness, that is, to redemption.

Human ideas of redemption have a development and a history and this history, as always, has been interpreted and misinterpreted as long as men, in ignorance of the will-guilt problem lying at their roots, played the one of the two factors against the other instead of recognizing them in their essential relationship and interaction. Redemption, according to the constellation of this conflict can relate now to will, another time to guilt, and finally also to consciousness. In relation to the time problem, however, will, guilt and consciousness maintain themselves differently, for the will, however one comprehends or interprets it, remains a constantly operating force, while consciousness above all is a quality, a state, and as such is passive and temporary, yes momentary. The feeling of pain, which manifests itself psychically as guilt feeling, arises from the attempts to unite these two incommensurable powers. In order to understand all the possibilities arising here in their historical development as well as individually, we must insert again a bit of will psychology and trace the opposing effect of the three factors, will, consciousness, and guilt feeling upon one another. The problem is considerably complicated, but is for the first time psychologically interesting through the fact that the will in the different levels of development through which it goes from the negative to the positive and creative, reacts upon the individual himself, upon what he has overcome and become.

In the relation of will to consciousness there is a naïve phase of development in which the two are one, as once probably the conscious individual will was one with the biological life impulse which it only represented and affirmed. The first developmental phase of the individual will, as it manifests itself in counter-will, corresponds to a "not willing," because one must; the second phase, that of positive will expression, corresponds to a "willing" what one must; the third creative phase, to a willing of that which one wants. The first phase corresponds to consciousness that one wills (against the compulsion of the other will); the second phase to a contentual knowing of that which one wills (because one must); the third creative phase binds the ego consciousness to the first with the positive will expression of the second, but corresponds in content not to a "must," but to a "self willed." On the first level, we perceive guilt feeling as a consequence of counter-will; on the second level we have guilt consciousness because we deny the own will, since we interpret willing as compulsion, we will, either not knowing what we will (content repression or rationalization) or that we will at all (dynamic denial). The third level, finally, creates guilt through conscious affirmation and expression of the own will and its personal content.

Thus consciousness and guilt which originally cooperate in the service of the negative will expression and the creative will achievement, finally place themselves inhibitingly in the way of will itself, yes call a halt to human will as such in neurotic guilt consciousness. All man's longing for happiness and redemption corresponds then to a spontaneous therapeutic attempt either to unite harmoniously once more this insoluble opposition of will and consciousness that manifests itself as consciousness of guilt or to separate them entirely. Both must miscarry. In the harmonious union, in the working together of will with consciousness which affirms the will, we sense, it is true, the feeling of happiness, but this can only be brief in duration and its lengthening can never be attained in continuous consciousness, therefore redemption is sought in unconsciousness, which involves a separation of the feeling of happiness from the temporal form of consciousness. Accordingly we have ever after the tendency to make-eternal which manifests itself in the different spheres of will, consciousness and guilt, whether we would immortalize pleasure in emotion, self consciousness in truth or the ego in creative work. All these self perpetuation tendencies correspond to the positive beneficent spontaneous therapies as we trace them in religious and love emotions on the one hand, in creative knowledge and artistic creation on the other. They do not all lead to redemption, however, because they always depend on the affirmation of consciousness and accordingly are limited temporally.

The actual redemption ideas which aim at eternal duration and a deliverance from consciousness can only be understood through guilt feeling, to the overcoming of which belongs release from will just as much as release from consciousness because it is just from the opposing reactions of these two that the tormenting self consciousness arises. The effect of guilt feeling on the conscious will extends from will restraint in the ethical sense beyond the crippling of will of the neurotic to the denial of will as Schopenhauer above all others has described it in all its appearances, including the destruction of will in self murder. Both exhaustively and magnificently the same philosopher has handled the eternal longing of man for salvation from this tormenting will. But Schopenhauer has been driven by emphasis on the guilt problem into pessimism, like Freud who finally followed him in this, so that there is no redemption except that of eternal nirvana, which Freud interpreted biologically as death instinct. This solution of the will problem to which Schopenhauer as we know was led by the Hindu religious philosophy, corresponded to the Hindu soul, which in the Buddhistic doctrine constituted the highest deification of human consciousness, and its ideal of redemption accordingly pictures a release from an overcoming by consciousness through the all powerful will. Schopenhauer, from the emphasis on guilt feeling, to which the Hindus give expression in the doctrine of transmigration of souls, has carried over his longing for salvation from consciousness to the will. Freud finally valued consciousness at first as a releasing source of healing against the sexual will in order finally to strike against guilt feeling as the insuperable obstacle. Nietzsche, who sought neither philosophic truth nor therapeutic illusions, but presented himself creatively, had the advantage of finding in the affirming will expression of self creation, the only redemption from will. For the neurotic human type, however, who suffers from consciousness and guilt feeling, salvation is to be found only in will denial as he can no longer find it in the temporary abrogation of consciousness in ecstatic states (and such is the creative act of will also). With him then the desire for redemption relates to the will to live in Schopenhauer's sense, to the instinct for life in Freud's meaning, speaking psychologically, to the will itself, but only because he cannot get free from the knowledge of it and the guilt consciousness following therefrom.

This leads then to the real task of individual psychotherapy, whose chief difficulty for me—like that of education—seems to lie in this, that both parties with their different psychologies have correspondingly different goals. On the level of individual therapy this opposition is shown in the fact that therapist and patient have a different salvation ideology. The therapist, as the strong will type who wants to create man in his own image, like the educator, sees salvation in getting loose, in the freeing from the compulsion of the evil will, whose self creative affirmation he denies at the same time in the therapeutic ideology of helping; the guilt springing therefrom he tries to dissipate through release from willing. The neurotic patient, on the contrary, who already suffers from will denial which he can no longer idealize through any illusion seeks not release from will but from consciousness which torments him in the form of guilt consciousness. He no longer wants to know, to know otherwise or better, but not to know at all, much more needs to be brought through emotional experience to positive will expression and affirmation, while the therapist just the reverse seeks the release from creative will in conscious knowledge. Since I reserve for another connection the further presentation and development of this contrast in the psychology of the helper and the patient, so important for the therapy and theory of the neuroses,[1] I now turn again to the universal spontaneous therapies as they lie before us in the happiness and redemption ideologies of humanity. For the same contrast in the psychology of both happiness and redemption-seeking individuals as we discover it in the artificial therapeutic situation, is maintained in the universal therapeutic power which the sexual and love life of men has become in the course of evolution. Here both sexes enjoy the beneficent feeling of will accomplishment, corresponding to the individual and sexual personality, but they find also release from individual consciousness in the temporary ecstatic self-forgetting of sensuous delirium and emotional yielding, and finally free themselves from guilt through the creation of the child as a generic function which is then transformed into an individual creation in bringing it up.

This blessedness through harmonious working together of all three spheres is found, however, only in the ideal love experience, which is not only limited in time as is all experience of happiness, but for the most part only endures for a brief period, as it shatters in the conflict of the two individual wills. As happiness means the consciousness of will attainment, it is not only brief in accordance with its own nature, but also is bound to reality, that is, to the overcoming of an external obstacle, a resistance, while redemption seeks a purely inner state of equal importance, which shall make the ego independent of the outer world. With the attempt of the individual to make the short-lived condition of happiness lasting, that is "saving," the pleasure quality is not only withdrawn from it as already pointed out, but the external resistance belonging to it is made permanent. In the individual love experience, which owes its possibility only to a favorable conjunction of the most diverse factors, the difficulty just pointed out manifests itself in this way, that the strange will finally becomes an external representative of the own counter-will instead of leading to an inner dissipation of it. In other words, the inner dualism showing itself as opposition between the racial sexual instinct and the conscious individual will, finds in the duality of the sexes only an external symbol—not the reverse.

[1] See "Will Therapy," Book II.

That is to say, the dualism of the self conscious individual no longer rests on the developmental level of bisexuality lying behind it for aeons, which would let us sleep peacefully if we had not developed in ourselves as consequence of the will-guilt conflict, the will to conquer the other and the longing for will subjection in emotional yielding, which we then interpret from within the will psychology in terms of sexual ideology as masculine and feminine.

The shattering of the human longing for happiness and redemption even in its highest individualistic form, in the love experience, leads finally to a form of salvation characteristic of the modern man, which I would like to designate quite generally as "therapeutic." [1] Therewith it becomes clear that this salvation tendency concerns guilt consciousness, for the making happy of the other releases from guilt and thus makes the individual himself happy. This therapeutic redemption ideology characterizes not only the love life of our time which itself is only an expression of it, but alone makes intelligible the meaning of individual psychotherapy of our present cultural life. For on the one side we see the particular person in search of salvation shatter on this individualized Christian sacrifice ideology; while on the other hand the modern type of psychotherapist who gradually succeeds the priest, has to thank the same ideology of redemption-of-the-other for his origin and steady growth. And while we previously found in the difference of the redemption ideologies of patient and therapist, a difficulty for successful treatment, here the fundamental likeness of their psychic structure, however positively and negatively expressed, proves to be a hindrance.

The neurotic type suffers in this, that he seeks to realize his longing for salvation only in the beatification of the other, for that is the form adequate to the modern man, in which the individual seeks release from his guilt; just so, however, it is the right form for the psychotherapist to seek his release from will in helping, in sacrifice for the other. However, the gratification which both strive for cannot be won in this way, but only through positive will accomplishment, while salvation is attainable in general only independently of the object. This mixture of happi-

[1] Compare the introductory conclusions of Book I in "Will Therapy."

ness and salvation-need, as it manifests itself clearly only in the therapeutic situation, is the characteristic mark of modern type who was described as neurotic. As he negates happiness, which the individual will affirmation is, in consequence of ethical will denial, he must upset the individual love therapy of which he is still capable only in terms of the just described salvation ideology of sacrifice for the other. In other words, he seeks to transform the possibility of happiness which lies in will achievement in opposition to the other, into a moralistic justification of will through the other, on the basis of which alone he could (for the first time) accept happiness. Thus the love relation with the modern neurotic type has become a moralistic, yes, if you will, a religious problem, at least in the psychological sense of the word, as he can no longer experience directly and immediately the possibility of happiness which lies in the love experience because of ethical will conflict, but must transform it into an individual release from moralistic compulsion. The love emotion of the modern neurotic is not a powerful will affirmation which leads to a feeling of happiness, but a therapeutic attempt at saving from the compulsion of the will-guilt conflict with the help of the other who as a rule is himself no therapist and hopes for the same release.

After the shattering of the universal redemption therapies, as they appear notably in religion with all its ramifications in art, philosophy and science, individual salvation for which the modern type strives, is to be found only in individual happiness, but this cannot be accepted because of the ethical guilt conflict of the individual. Love, whose failure as individual redemption therapy is now evident, was the last attempt to transform the individual possibility of happiness with the other into an individual salvation through the other. While happiness can only be found individually and then also means individual redemption, in its essence redemption is only to be found universally because it comes to a climax just in the abrogation of individuality. If individuation has advanced so far that the individual can no longer find salvation in the universal through the universal ideologies, but must seek them individually, then there remains no other possibility of salvation except the release from individual self consciousness in death. This destructive form of salvation as it is manifested in the growing tendency to suicide of the modern individual, represents indeed the greatest victory of the individual will over the life impulse and all ethical inhibitions, but no longer works therapeutically, not even when, as in psychoanalytic theory, it is presented in the scientific garb of a death instinct. For with men even the biological factors are placed in large measure under the control of will and thus certainly are also exposed to the danger of manifesting themselves destructively because of the guilt problem. We know just from psychoanalytic experiences that men can sicken and die when they will it, that, however, just as often in a miraculous fashion they can escape death—if they will it. It is just this conflict of the individual will with the biological compulsive forces that constitutes the essentially human problem, in its creative as in its destructive manifestations.

If the will is affirmed and not negated or denied, there results the life instinct, and happiness, like salvation, is found in life and experience, in the creation and acceptance of both without having to ask how, whither, what and why. Questions which originate from the division of will into guilt consciousness and self consciousness cannot be answered through any psychological or philosophic theory for the answer is the more disillusioning, the more correct it is. For happiness can only be found in reality, not in truth, and redemption never in reality and from reality, but only in itself and from itself.

COMPLETE LIST OF PUBLISHED WORKS
OF DR. OTTO RANK

IN ORDER OF THEIR FIRST PUBLICATION

Der Künstler, 1907

Der Mythus der Geburt des Heldens, 1909. English translation, *The Myth of the Birth of the Hero*, 1914. Italian translation, 1921

Ein Traum der Selbst deutet. Jahrbuch für Psa II, 1910. *Psychoanalytic Review*, Vol. V, 1918

Die Lohengrin Sage, 1911

Das Inzestmotiv in Dichtung und Sage, 1912. Revised edition 1926. French translation, 1934

Die Bedeutung der Psychoanalyse für die Geisteswissenschaften (with H. Sachs), 1913. English translation, 1915. Nervous and Mental Disease Monograph Series.

Psychoanalytische Beiträge zur Mythenforschung: Gesammelte Studien aus den Jahren 1912–14, 1919; revised edition 1922.

Der Doppelgänger, in *Imago*, 1914. In pamphlet form 1925. *Psychoanalytic Review*, Vol. VI, 1919

Homer: Psychologische Beiträge zur Entstehungsgeschichte des Volksepos, in *Imago V*, 1917

Das Volksepos: Die dichterische Phantasiebildung, in *Imago V*, 1917

Don Juan-Gestalt, in *Imago VIII*, 1922. In book form, 1924. *Psychoanalytic Review*, Vol. XIII, 1926. French translation, 1932

Eine Neurosenanalyse in Träumen, 1924

Sexualität und Schuldgefühl, 1926. Translation: *Perversion and Neurosis, International Journal of Psychoanalysis* IV. 270

Entwicklungsziele der Psychoanalyse (with S. Ferenczi), 1924. English translation, *The Development of Psychoanalysis*, 1925

COMPLETE LIST OF PUBLISHED WORKS

Das Trauma der Geburt, 1924. French translation, 1928. English translation, *The Trauma of Birth*, 1929

Technik der Psychoanalyse. Vol. I, 1926. Vol. II, 1929. Vol. III, 1931. English translation, *Will Therapy*, 1936

Grundzüge einer genetischen Psychologie auf Grund der Psychoanalyse der Ich-Struktur. Vol. I, *Genetische Psychologie*, 1927. (Given in lecture form in English for the New York School of Social Work, 1926.) Translations: *Genesis of Genitality*, in *Psychoanalytic Review* XII, 1921; *Psychoanalytic Problems*, in *Psychoanalytic Review* XIV, 1927. Vol. II, *Gestaltung und Ausdruck der Persönlichkeit*, 1928. (Given in lecture form for the New York School of Social Work and the Pennsylvania School of Social Work, 1927.) Translations: *Introduction: Beyond Psychoanalysis*, in *Psychoanalytic Review* XVI, 1929; *Character-formation* and *The Task of Education*, pamphlet, New York Committee for Mental Hygiene. Vol. III, *Wahrheit und Wirklichkeit*, 1929. (Given in lecture form for the Pennsylvania School of Social Work, 1929.) English translation: *Truth and Reality*, 1936

Seelenglaube und Psychologie, 1931

Modern Education, 1931

Art and Artist, 1932

Beyond Psychology. Posthumous, privately printed, 1941